Castles of Edward the First in Wales

P H Humphries

First published 1983

ISBN 0 11 790262 4

Contents

Acknowledgements

All illustrations are Crown copyright except for the following:

Author: 4, 10, 11, 20, 21, 22, 23, 28, 29, 31, 32, 41, 57

British Library: 14, 18, 19

Public Record Office: 3, 25

Wales Tourist Board: 2, 15

Royal Library Windsor: 5 *(Reproduced by gracious permission of Her Majesty the Queen)*

Abram Public Relations: 6

Studio Jon, Fishguard: 13

National Library of Wales: 33

R Avent: 55

1 *Wales before the Edwardian conquest*
1 *Cymru cyn concwest Edward*
1 *Le Pays de Galles avant la conquête du roi Edouard Ier*
1 *Wales vor Eroberung durch Edward I.*

Introduction

Between 1277 and 1295, King Edward I created in Wales a magnificent series of military masterpieces in stone, without rival in these islands. Their construction was a carefully organised state enterprise, their fortifications were the most advanced of their day and the record of their building is the fullest for any group of structures at that period.

During those eighteen years, the King founded here no fewer than nine major new royal castles, all of them linked to town boroughs. He repaired four captured Welsh castles, together with others on the English side of the border and, in addition, he persuaded his marcher lords to build four castles in their own territories at their own expense. It was no mean achievement, even for a king.

Although they are ruined now, these castles have bequeathed to Wales a legacy of splendour that has made the country renowned throughout the world. The cause of their building was a simple one of warfare, but the underlying reasons for it are rather more complex.

2 *The great seal of Llywelyn ab Iorwerth*
2 *Sêl fawr Llywelyn ab Iorwerth*
2 *Le grand sceau de Llywelyn ab Iorwerth*
2 *Das Große Siegel von Llywelyn ab Iorwerth*

Background

Wales, before the Edwardian conquest, was a geographical rather than a political entity. It had long been divided into separate kingdoms, each ruled by independent princely families and there was no acknowledged supreme ruler. During the course of time, however, the princes of the north-western kingdom of Gwynedd won gradual acceptance as national leaders. Partly, this was due to their natural stronghold of Snowdonia, partly to their control over the agricultural grainlands of Anglesey; but, in the thirteenth century, it was due mainly to the personalities of the princes of Gwynedd, Llywelyn ab Iorwerth (The Great) and his grandson, Llywelyn ap Gruffydd (The Last).

Llywelyn ab Iorwerth

Llywelyn ab Iorwerth gained supremacy in Gwynedd around 1200 and soon managed to turn the conflicts in King John's England to his own advantage, winning for himself virtual control of independent north and west Wales. In his rise to power, he had dispossessed his own rival kith and kin and overturned the Welsh laws of equal inheritance, but he took good care, from the first, to satisfy English law by doing homage to the king of England, as his predecessors had done before him. The concept of homage was extremely important in the middle ages – it was a vital part of the feudal system of land tenure and it implied a direct overlordship. Ever since AD 878, during the time of Alfred the Great, Welsh princes had been accustomed to swear some form of shadowy allegiance to the kings of England; however, once Owain Gwynedd had done homage to King Henry II in 1157, this too was to become an obligatory duty upon them. Indeed, it was this very failure to render homage which eventually drove King Edward I to go to war in Wales.

Llywelyn ap Gruffydd

Llywelyn the Great's attempt to ensure single succession for his hard-won conquests eventually came to nought. Wales was once more divided and the English hold tightened, through control of the four cantrefs of land between the rivers Conwy and Dee. Around 1255, a second Llywelyn came to the fore in Gwynedd – Llywelyn ap Gruffydd, a grandson of Llywelyn the Great. He too had risen to power by ousting his brothers from their rightful inheritance and he possessed many of the qualities of leadership and statecraft that had been apparent in his grandfather. Across the border, England was soon to become embroiled in civil war, between King Henry III and his barons, and Llywelyn was quick to seize this opportunity to ally himself with the baronial leader, Simon de Montfort. By the end of the conflict, Llywelyn had achieved total

3

3 *The Treaty of Montgomery, 1267*
3 *Cytundeb Trefaldwyn, 1267*
3 *Le Traité de Montgomery, 1267*
3 *Frieden zu Montgomery 1267*

4

4 *Llywelyn ap Gruffydd: statue of c. 1916 in Cardiff City Hall*
4 *Llywelyn ap Gruffydd: cerflun o c. 1916 yn Neuadd y Ddinas, Caerdydd*
4 *Llywelyn ap Gruffydd: statue de 1916 du City Hall de Cardiff*
4 *Llywelyn ap Gruffydd: Statue von ca. 1916, City Hall in Cardiff*

5

5 Edward I and Llywelyn ap Gruffydd in parliament: fictitious drawing of 1534

5 Edward I a Llywelyn ap Gruffydd mewn trafodaeth: darlun dychmygol o 1534

5 Edouard Ier et Llywelyn ap Gruffydd au parlement : dessin imaginaire de 1534

5 Edward I. und Llywelyn ap Gruffydd im Parlament (Phantasiezeichnung von 1534)

superiority in Wales and King Henry could do little more than come to terms with him. At the Treaty of Montgomery, in 1267, England formally recognised Llywelyn ap Gruffydd as Prince of Wales, granting him the homages of other Welsh princes, upon condition of his making an annual payment to the English crown, and returning the Four Cantrefs once more to Welsh control.

For a few years Llywelyn rode the crest of a wave, but in 1272 King Henry III died. Although Henry's son, the Lord Edward (now to become King Edward I), was abroad, the Welsh prince had encountered him already, as governor of the Four Cantrefs and he had reason to doubt this new king's intentions; perhaps rashly, he decided to halt his agreed payments to the English Crown. In 1273, with Edward still away, the king's regents wrote to the Prince of Wales forbidding him to erect his new castle of Dolforwyn, in Powys; Llywelyn replied that although he might hold his principality under royal power, his rights within it were his own affair. His answer illustrates how differently both parties viewed their respective positions.

Causes for War

King Edward I returned to England in 1274 to take up the reins of government. Throughout most of that year the Prince of Wales was preoccupied in trying to uncover a local plot upon his life: he excused himself from attending the king's coronation and did not render homage to him as he was required to do. After the discovery of the assassination plot, the main conspirators, one of whom was Llywelyn's own brother Dafydd, fled to England, where they were immediately granted protection by the king. Now all the prince's former suspicions were turned into outright hostility. To King Edward's summons he replied that he would neither do homage nor continue his payments until these fugitives were returned to Wales, and he made further conditions that he should receive satisfaction over outstanding border disputes and that the king should endorse the Treaty of Montgomery.

It was now a question of principle on both sides. For his part, Edward I was determined to make the act of homage the main issue, for he could not lightly disregard it. He was punctilious, but unrelenting; he sent the prince three further summonses to appear before him in England and, on each occasion, Llywelyn sent envoys with letters of excuse. One more factor now contributed to the impending onset of war. Llywelyn suddenly arranged to marry Eleanor, the daughter of Simon de Montfort. King Edward was determined to prevent any possible revival of a baronial faction and so he had her taken prisoner as she was coming by sea to Wales. The prince was incensed and became still more obdurate in his defiance.

By November 1276, the king's patience was exhausted. At a full meeting of magnates and prelates, it was announced that he should *accept no further excuses, but should go against the said Llywelyn as a rebel and disturber of his peace.*

6 *King Edward I: statue at Lincoln Cathedral*
6 *Y Brenin Edward I: cerflun yn Eglwys Gadeiriol Lincoln*
6 *Le Roi Edouard Ier : statue de la Cathédrale de Lincoln*
6 *König Edward I.: Statue in der Kathedrale zu Lincoln*

England and Wales at war

First Campaign

The first Edwardian campaign was a short, methodical affair. Throughout the initial eight months, the king was busy subduing the princes of southern parts of Wales and so cutting away support for Llywelyn. In July 1277, he took to the field, moving, with his army, from Chester along the north Wales coast and towards the prince's stronghold of Snowdonia. At one time, the English army numbered as many as 15,000 men: it included not only Llywelyn's fugitive brother Dafydd, who was fighting with the king, but up to 9,000 foot-soldiers from the English controlled parts of south Wales. The first line consisted of teams of wood-cutters to hew a broad path through the dense forests. As the army passed through it carefully secured communications to the rear by building strongholds, first at Flint and then at Rhuddlan. In the south meanwhile, advancing support forces created two further bases at Builth and Aberystwyth. By September, Edward had progressed as far as Deganwy, on the Conwy estuary and, from there, he sent his fleet to take Anglesey and gather its grain harvest, upon which Llywelyn depended for his continued survival.

The Prince of Wales was unable to shake off his adversary and, with his food supply now cut off, he sued for peace. For his part, too, King Edward must have been unwilling to risk a troublesome winter campaign in the mountains and so terms were drawn up in November, at the Treaty of Aberconwy. Llywelyn was now humbled, but he was not crushed; stripped of most of his former rights and possessions, he was compelled to render homage to the king. Edward himself made provision for Dafydd, who had been his ally in war and to whom he had promised Llywelyn's lands of Snowdonia, by granting him the two most

7

7 Edward's army on the march: imaginative drawing by D L Owen
7 Byddin Edward yn ymdeithio: darlun dychmygol gan D L Owen
7 L'armée d'Edouard en marche : dessin imaginaire de D L Owen
7 Edwards Armee auf dem Vormarsch (Zeichnung von D. L. Owen)

southerly of the Four Cantrefs. Finally, in 1278, Llywelyn was permitted to marry Eleanor de Montfort at Worcester and the king himself presided over the celebrations.

Castles of the First Campaign

The first war left four new English royal castles of major importance in Wales. It had been the king's policy to secure his gains with firm bases before advancing to his next objective and these bases – at Aberystwyth, Builth, Flint and Rhuddlan – which had been of wood to begin with, were now completed in stone at all possible speed. Together with two lesser foundations at Ruthin, which was initially a royal castle, and Hawarden, apparently a lordship castle from the first, these castles continued to be held by the king's agents throughout the period after the first war.

Second Campaign

After the Aberconwy settlement, a feeling of resentment began slowly to manifest itself beneath the country's peaceful façade. In the first place, there was Llywelyn's disaffected brother Dafydd, who had now changed sides four times and had done his utmost to injure his brother in the past; having had to make do with two cantrefs instead of his promised lands of Snowdonia, he now felt he had deserved more. The men of the two northern cantrefs had the most genuine grievance; they had seen their forests cut down, their customs and privileges violated and their Welsh laws

8 Aberystwyth Castle
8 Castell Aberystwyth
8 Le Château d'Aberystwyth
8 Aberystwyth Castle

8

9

9 *Builth Castle from the air*
9 *Castell Llanfair-ym-Muallt o'r awyr*
9 *Vue aérienne de Builth Castle*
9 *Builth Castle aus der Vogelschau*

disregarded. Llywelyn, for his part, however, seems to have been prepared to make the best of his new position, although he must still have smarted at the injury to his pride and prestige.

In the end, it was Dafydd who kindled the flame of rebellion that led to the second war. On Palm Sunday 1282, he swooped down on the castle of Hawarden in the dead of night, overpowered its garrison and took prisoner its governor. He then set about raising the whole country in rebellion. Placed on the horns of a dilemma over whether or not to support the uprising, Llywelyn elected to join his brother and so to provide a focus of leadership for his countrymen. Within two days, the Welsh had taken the new castle of Aberystwyth and driven back the English in large parts of south and west Wales.

Forced to join battle once again, King Edward I now adopted similar tactics to those he had employed in the first Welsh war. His three armies effected a pincer movement, aimed at blockading Llywelyn's stronghold of Snowdonia, but the Welsh enjoyed some successes in minor engagements and were not to be so easily beaten. From Anglesey, the king's troops built a bridge of boats over to the mainland near Bangor then, attempting to cross, they were set upon and annihilated.

Death of Llywelyn

Llywelyn realised the danger of an English blockade on Snowdonia and was determined to avoid a recurrence of the disaster of 1277. He therefore made his way south, where resistance was flagging, to create a diversion and relieve pressure on Gwynedd. In November he appeared in Builth, in an effort to capture the castle there and it was this endeavour that was finally to be his undoing. On 11 December 1282 Llywelyn ap Gruffydd, Prince of north Wales, was killed in a small engagement at Irfon Bridge, near Builth. The man whose lance struck him down, one Stephen Frankton, did not recognise whom he had killed and it was only afterwards that the prince's identity was discovered and the news brought quickly to the king.

10

10 *Hawarden Castle*
10 *Castell Penarlâg*
10 *Château de Hawarden*
10 *Hawarden Castle*

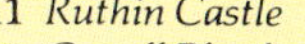

11 *Ruthin Castle*
11 *Castell Rhuthun*
11 *Château de Ruthin*
11 *Ruthin Castle*

BEAUMARIS
(1295)
CONWY
RHUDDLAN
FLINT
HAWARDEN
DENBIGH
CHESTER
CAERNARFON
RUTHIN
HOPE
HOLT
NORTHERN ARMY
DOLWYDDELAN
CRICCIETH
HARLECH
SHREWSBURY
CASTELL Y BERE
CASTLES OF THE EDWARDIAN CAMPAIGNS
MONTGOMERY
CENTRAL ARMY
ABERYSTWYTH
CARDIGAN
BUILTH
HEREFORD
CARMARTHEN
SOUTHERN ARMY

13

Llywelyn's death proved decisive. Only he could give life to the struggle; he left no heir and, without his leadership, the Welsh quickly lost heart. Edward I now hunted Dafydd remorselessly, mopping up pockets of resistance as he went and, by June 1283, it was all over. Dafydd was given up by his own countrymen; he was tried at Shrewsbury and executed as a traitor.

Costs of the Wars

This time, the king was determined not merely to control the Welsh, but to prevent any possible recurrence of such a war in Wales. The struggle had cost him dearly – £23,000 for the first campaign and around £80,000 for the second, which had involved a long winter engagement. Multiplying by about 600, or more, this would be equivalent to £60m or £70m all told, at 1983 values and it had had to be financed on borrowed money – provided by the wealthy merchants of northern Italy, who acted as bankers of the day. Had the king's credit with the Italians not been good in those years, his success in Wales would have been impossible. As it was, troubles were looming on the horizon in Scotland and in his lands of Gascony, so that Edward could not afford another major war in Wales. His solutions to the problem were part political and part military; both were to have the most far-reaching effects upon the country's future.

Political Settlement

On the political front, the king was resolved to end the often bitter disputes which had dogged his reign so far. Gwynedd was now to be annexed to the English crown; it was divided into the counties of Anglesey, Caernarvonshire, Merionethshire and Flintshire, each to be administered from one of the new castles. The laws, by which these additional crown lands were to be governed, were laid down in the Great Statute of Wales, a remarkable document for its time, issued at Rhuddlan on 19 March 1284.

14

12 Edward I's second campaign in Wales
12 Ail ymgyrch Edward I yng Nghymru
12 Seconde campagne d'Edouard Ier au Pays de Galles
12 2. Feldzug von Edward I. in Wales

13 Nineteenth-century memorial stone at Cilmeri, near Builth
13 Cofeb o'r bedwaredd ganrif ar bymtheg yng Nghilmeri, ger Llanfair-ym-Muallt
13 Pierre commémorative du dix-neuvième siècle de Cilmeri près de Builth
13 Gedenkstein aus dem 19. Jhdt. in Cilmeri bei Builth

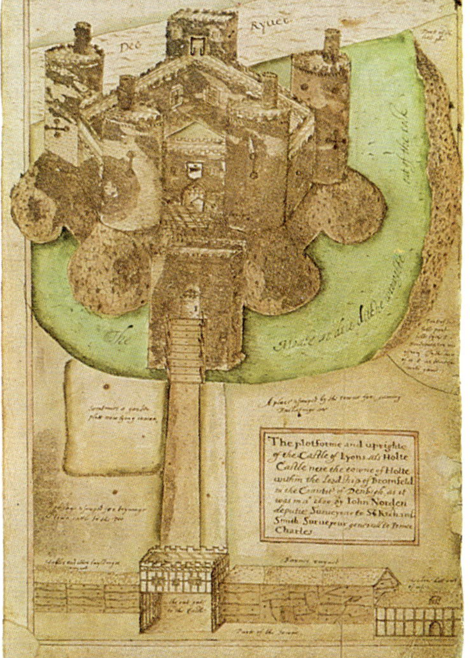

14 Holt Castle in 1620: drawing by John Norden
14 Castell Holt ym 1620: darlun gan John Norden
14 Château de Holt en 1620: dessin de John Norden
14 Holt Castle im Jahre 1620 (Zeichnung: John Norden)

15 *Chirk Castle*
15 *Castell y Waun*
15 *Château de Chirk*
15 *Chirk Castle*

Castles of the Second Campaign

It was King Edward's military settlement for Wales that provided, and to this day provides, still, such a dramatic visual impact. His plan was as bold in its conception as it was costly in its execution. Snowdonia was to be bound around by an iron ring of castles, each having access by sea, so that never again could it become a focal point of insurrection and a last bastion of resistance. These major defence works along the coast – at Conwy, Caernarfon, Harlech and at the former Welsh castle of Criccieth – were backed up by inland fortifications; Welsh castles at Dolwyddelan, Castell y Bere and Caergwrle (Hope) were repaired and re-garrisoned whilst, towards the English border, the marcher lords were persuaded to build their own defences at Denbigh, Holt and Chirk. The total cost of these building works to the English Exchequer was somewhere around £80,000 but, even so, this was less than the cost of the two military campaigns in Wales. By and large, they kept the peace for the following 100 years and the king would probably have considered his investment to be worthwhile.

16 *Organisation of labour for castle building in Wales, 1282*
16 *Trefnu gweithwyr ar gyfer adeiladu cestyll yng Nghymru, 1282*

The Castles

King Edward's military success in Wales was gained largely through his creation of an army of almost national proportions out of the miscellaneous forces available to him. At this period, the statutory 40 days' feudal service under arms was still the normal means of raising troops; the king's achievement lay in his widespread adoption of paid military service to supplement these short-term feudal arrangements.

Labour Force

As with his army, so with his castle building; this too was accomplished by the extensive use of conscription and paid labour. Within a month of the outbreak of the second war, in 1282, summonses were on their way to every part of England, Ireland and the English possessions in France, calling for the provision of materials and labour to follow the king into Wales. About 2,500 woodcutters, carpenters, diggers and masons were pressed into service from the English shires alone — almost every county having to provide its quota. The main assembly point was Chester and most of them — like a group of 70 men who left Newport Pagnell with a handcart for their tools — travelled there on foot. When they arrived, they were marshalled into organised parties to follow in the wake of the main army. During the 1277 campaign, almost 3,000 workmen had been similarly conscripted and many of these, the masons in particular, were almost certainly still employed in Wales in 1282. Out of a total population in the country at that time of only three or four million people, the organisation of so much mobile labour must have represented a sizeable proportion of the entire workforce.

The Architect

The man in charge of the building operations was Master James of St George, a master mason from

Impressment of workmen for the King's Works in North Wales 1282–3

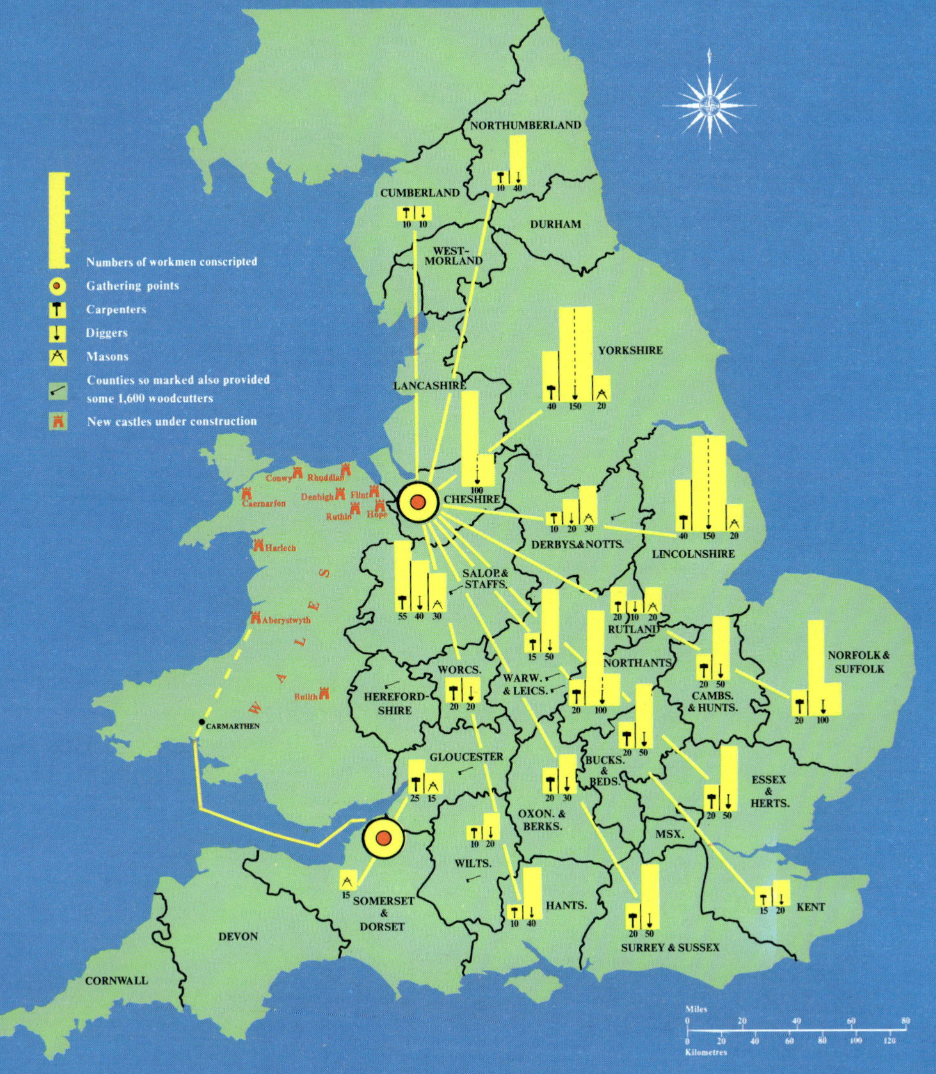

16

16 *Organisation de la main-d'oeuvre pour la construction d'un château au Pays de Galles, 1282*

16 *Organisation der Arbeiten zum Burgbau in Wales, 1282*

17 (overleaf) *Building workers receiving their pay: imaginative drawing by D L Owen*

17 (trosodd) *Adeiladwyr yn cael eu tâl: llun dychmygol gan D L Owen*

17 (voir au verso) *Ouvriers du bâtiment recevant leur paie : dessin fictif de D L Owen*

17 (umstehend) *Entlohnung der Bauleute (Phantasiezeichnung von D. L. Owen)*

18 (overleaf) *A king and his master mason: drawing of c.1250 by Matthew Paris*

18 (trosodd) *Brenin a'i brif fasiwn: darlun o c. 1250 gan Matthew Paris*

18 (voir au verso) *Un roi et son maître maçon : dessin de 1250 de Matthew Paris*

18 (umstehend) *Ein König und sein Baumeister (Zeichnung von Matthew Paris, ca. 1250)*

17

18

19 Fifteenth century French drawing showing helicoidal (spiral) scaffolding
19 Darlun Ffrengig o'r bymthegfed ganrif yn dangos sgaffaldiau helicoidal (troellog)
19 Dessin francais du quinzième siècle indiquant un échaffaudage hélicoïdal (En spirale)
19 Französische Zeichnung, 15. Jhdt: Spiralförmiges Gerüst

Savoy (on the French border with Switzerland and Italy) who seems to have possessed quite exceptional qualities. Edward I must have met him initially on a visit he made to Savoy in 1273; at the time Master James had been engaged in building a series of great castles for the counts of Savoy at places such as Yverdon and St Georges d'Espéranche (from where he took his name) and these must greatly have impressed the new king of England. At any rate, from April 1278, we find Master James working in north Wales, where he is soon referred to as the Master of the King's Works and drawing a high daily wage of two shillings – equivalent to the average weekly rate for an ordinary mason.

The Savoy Connection

The office of master mason, in the middle ages, was akin to that of architect today. He was responsible for the overall design of a building as well as for superintending its construction. Several such senior posts in Wales, under Edward I, were given to craftsmen from Savoy and it is not, therefore, surprising to find similarities in architectural detail between the castles of Savoy and the Edwardian fortresses in Wales: details such as the frequent use of helicoidal (spiralled) scaffolding in building round towers (indicated by corresponding holes in the masonry); the common occurrence of the Norman style half-round arch; the positioning, at Harlech and Rhuddlan, of latrine shafts as shallow buttress-like projections at the junction of tower and inner curtain wall; the decoration, at Conwy, of the battlements with triple stone pinnacles; the distinctive type of window design in the principal rooms at Harlech; and a diagonal inner angle where a corner tower joins the inner curtain walls. These six features rarely occur elsewhere in the British Isles.

19

21

20 Conwy, Watch Tower: showing holes left by helicoidal scaffolding
20 Conwy, Tŵr y Gwyliwr: yn dangos tyllau a adawyd gan y sgaffaldiau troellog
20 Tour de guet de Conwy : traces de trous laissés par l'échaffaudage hélicoïdal
20 Conwy, Wachtturm: Löcher für Spiralgerüste sind sichtbar

21 Harlech Castle: latrine shaft in north-west corner
21 Castell Harlech: siafft geudy yng nghornel y gogledd-orllewin
21 Château de Harlech : puits des latrines situé dans l'angle nord-ouest
21 Harlech Castle: Latrinenschaft in der NW-Ecke

Building Records

Edward I's castles are remarkable for the wealth of surviving contemporary record on the cost of their erection. Because that erection was financed entirely by the Crown, particulars of expenditure are still preserved in the documents at the Public Record Office. These have been the subject of much careful study over recent years, so that we now know such details as the names of the men who worked on these castles, how much money they were paid, how long the construction took and where all the materials came from.

20

22 Harlech Castle: window on top floor of gatehouse
22 Castell Harlech: ffenestr ar lawr uchaf y tŷ porth
22 Château de Harlech: fenêtre située au dernier étage du corps-de-garde
22 Harlech Castle: Fenster auf der obersten Etage des Torhauses

23 Conwy Castle: pinnacles on battlements of SW Tower
23 Castell Conwy: pinaclau ar furiau amddiffyn Tŵr y de-orllewin
23 Château de Conwy: pinacles de créneaux de la Tour SO
23 Conwy Castle: Zinnen auf der Festungsmauer des SW-Turms

Building Time

Building was a seasonal operation in the middle ages, carried on mainly between April and November. During the winter, the tops of unfinished walls would often be protected from frosts with a covering of thatch and only essential staff were retained on site. Of the eight major castles, those of Harlech, Builth, Aberystwyth, Flint, Rhuddlan and Conwy were all substantially completed in between five and seven building seasons, although Caernarfon, which was conceived on a grander scale, was under construction until 1339 and even then remained unfinished.

Transport of Materials

The provision of building materials and their transport to the site was a continuing commitment that demanded careful organisation. Most important of the necessary resources was money: without it, men could not be paid, materials could not be

24 Ships unloading building materials: imaginative drawing by D L Owen
24 Llongau'n dadlwytho defnyddiau adeiladu: darlun dychmygol gan D L Owen
24 Vaisseaux déchargeant des matériaux de construction : dessin imaginaire de D L Owen
24 Schiffe beim Entladen von Baumaterial (Phantasiezeichnung von D. L. Owen)

24

purchased and building would come to a halt. It had to come overland from places like London or York, or by sea from Ireland and all was in the form of silver pennies, the only unit of coinage, packed tight into wooden barrels for transportation.

Basic raw materials for the building work, such as stone, lime and sand, were usually taken from as close to the site as possible, although stone was required in differing qualities and often had to be brought from more than one quarry source.

Timber, of course, was needed in enormous quantities and often had to come from quite far afield. It was used for initial site stockades, for scaffolding and other construction needs, for floors and roofs and for timber framed buildings in the castles and their attached towns. It came by ship, at first from Liverpool and Chester and later from Rhuddlan and Conwy.

Glass for windows does not figure very often in the records, although it must have been used for many of the major buildings in these castles; usually it seems to have come from Chester.

Lead for roofs was mined in various English centres but, later on, it came from Flintshire and even Snowdonia. Lastly came iron, steel and tin – needed in great quantities for items such as nails, cramps and cables and for all the workmen's tools. Most of this seems to have come from Newcastle-under-Lyme, which was then an important centre of the metalworking trade.

Lordship Castles

The lordship castles of Denbigh, Chirk, Holt and Hawarden, illustrate the variation in our knowledge about royal and non-royal building works. These castles were built and paid for by the marcher lords within their own lordships, although their construction was part of the king's overall policy. Some of them had quite extensive fortifications – at Denbigh, for example, there was an entire walled town attached to a spacious castle – yet the records of their erection that have come down to us are, at best, somewhat sketchy and, at worst, non-existent.

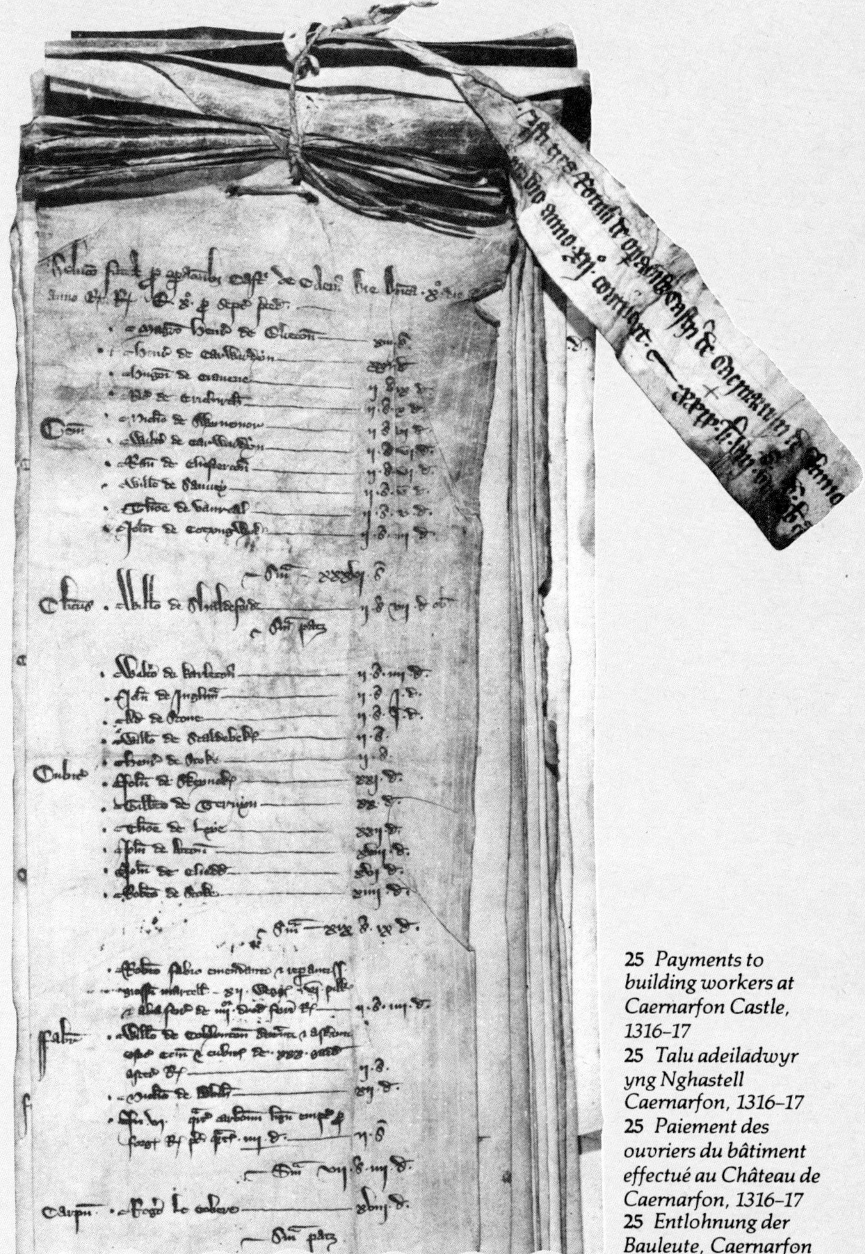

25

25 *Payments to building workers at Caernarfon Castle, 1316–17*
25 *Talu adeiladwyr yng Nghastell Caernarfon, 1316–17*
25 *Paiement des ouvriers du bâtiment effectué au Château de Caernarfon, 1316–17*
25 *Entlohnung der Bauleute, Caernarfon Castle, 1316–17*

26

26 *Denbigh Castle from the air*
26 *Castell Dinbych o'r awyr*
26 *Vue aérienne du Château de Denbigh*
26 *Denbigh Castle (Luftaufnahme)*

27 *Beaumaris Castle from the air: the ultimate in concentric planning*
27 *Castell Biwmares o'r awyr: yr eithaf mewn cynllunio consentrig*
27 *Vue aérienne du Château de Beaumaris : l'ultime en conception concentrique*
27 *Beaumaris Castle (Luftaufnahme); ein konzentrischer Bau, wie er im Buche steht.*

Defensive Planning

Edward I began building his castles in Wales when the development of stone fortification was just reaching its height. It was the age of the concentric castle, perfected a year or two earlier at Caerphilly in south Wales, where a high inner ward dominated a low outer enclosure and all was surrounded by water. Its advantages against conventional attack by force of arms were difficulty of access and lack of cover for any attacker, coupled with vastly increased firepower for the defenders. Where the nature of the site allowed, a concentric plan was adopted for most of Edward's new castles – Aberystwyth, Builth, Harlech, Rhuddlan and Beaumaris (this last, begun in 1295 after a rebellion) all made use of the walls within walls principle. At Flint, an unusual offset square arrangement was chosen, whilst Conwy and Caernarfon were both built on narrow outcrops of rock whose shape dictated a linear building plan. Apart from the inland site of Builth, all these other castles incorporated a means of access for shipping, so that they could be supplied and victualled by sea – an essential part of King Edward's initial strategy, which was often to prove a decisive factor in their later history. These Edwardian castles incorporated heavily defended gatehouses and massive curtain walls which, in some cases, were pierced by continuous passages for additional defence. The permanent garrisons which manned them, together with their towns, averaged around 30 in number and, at times, there were often far less than that. In the final analysis, the success of such small numbers is proof enough of the strength of Edward's great fortifications.

Defended Towns

It is to the towns that we turn last, for they played an equally important part in the king's plan for the settlement of Wales. In his lands of Gascony, in south west France, King Edward had become acquainted with, and indeed founded, many fortified towns, or *bastides*, and now he extended this same policy to the newly conquered territories in Wales. With the exception of the former Welsh

27

28

castle of Dolwyddelan and of Chirk and Hawarden, both in lordship areas, every other castle which Edward built in Wales at this time had attached to it a town borough. Some of these new boroughs were quite small, enclosed simply by earth banks and timber stockades; others did not survive very long, but at Denbigh and more especially at Conwy and Caernarfon, they were heavily defended with high stone walls, mural towers and gatehouses. The

28 *Harlech Castle: the main approach. A daunting prospect*
28 *Castell Harlech: y brif fynedfa. Golygfa echrydus.*
28 *Château de Harlech : voie d'accès principale. Perspective intimidante*
28 *Harlech Castle: Haupteingang – ein eindrucksvoller Anblick*

29 *Caernarfon Castle: three tiers of arrowloops in the south curtain wall*
29 *Castell Caernarfon: tair rhes o dyllau saethu yn y llenfur deheuol*
29 *Château de Caernarfon: trois rangées d'archères dans la courtine sud*
29 *Caernarfon Castle: drei Reihen von Schießscharten in der südlichen kurtine*

30 *Caernarfon Castle and walled town from the air*
30 *Castell Caernarfon, y dref a'i muriau o'r awyr*
30 *Vue aérienne du Château de Caernarfon et de l'enceinte de la ville*
30 *Caernarfon Castle und Stadtbefestigungen (Luftaufnahme)*

30

29

31 *Conwy: the town walls near the quay*
31 *Conwy: muriau'r dref gerllaw'r cei*
31 *Conwy : les murs de la ville près du quai*
31 *Conwy: Stadtmauer in der Nähe des Kais*

32 *Monpazier, south-west France: a fortified town founded by Edward I, 1284*
32 *Monpazier, de-orllewin Ffrainc: tref gaerog a sefydlwyd gan Edward I, 1284*
32 *Monpazier, sud-ouest de la France: ville fortifiée fondée par Edouard Ier, 1284*
32 *Monpazier, Südwest-Frankreich; von Edward I. 1284 gegründete Stadtbefestigung*

33 *Caernarfon in 1610: ground plan by John Speed*
33 *Caernarfon ym 1610: plan o'r llawr gan John Speed*
33 *Caernarfon en 1610 : section horizontale de John Speed*
33 *Caernarfon im Jahre 1610 (Grundriß von John Speed)*

31

32

latter two retain their walls almost intact and the streets that run through them today follow still the layout of medieval times.

Into these new towns the king attracted English merchants and traders to come and settle, protected safe behind their walls, by offering grants of land and valuable trading privileges. The Welsh people of the locality were welcome to come in by day and to trade, but they had to live outside the walls and these new towns became a source of much bitterness and resentment in the country. Gradually such social and national divisions were broken down through intermarriage. The increasing use of gunpowder, throughout the fourteenth and fifteenth centuries, began to render obsolete these carefully built defences of an earlier epoch and the walled towns lost their importance as time went by. With the accession of a Welshman, Henry Tudor, to the throne of England, these former garrison towns were thrown open to all and they quickly lost their English identity as they spread outside their ancient stone boundaries to face a new and freer age.

33

34 *Flint Castle: the north-east tower*
34 *Castell y Fflint: tŵr y gogledd-ddwyrain*
34 *Le château de Flint: la tour Nord-Est*
34 *Flint Castle: der nord-östl. Turm*

Flint Castle

35 *View from the East*
35 *Golygfa o'r dwyrain*
35 *Vue de l'Est*
35 *Ansicht von O*

36

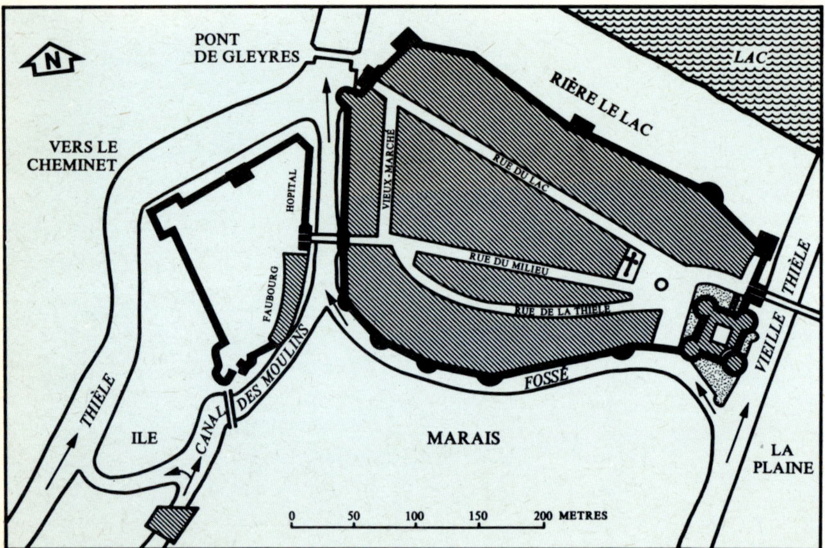

36 *Plan of Yverdon, Switzerland: the forerunner of Flint?*
36 *Yverdon, Y Swistir: rhagflaenydd y Fflint?*
36 *Yverdon, Suisse: le précurseur de Flint?*
36 *Yverdon, Schweiz — ein Muster für Flint?*

Flint and Rhuddlan were the two greatest castles of the first Welsh campaign of 1277. Between them, they were intended to bring under permanent control the long disputed northern territories of the Four Cantrefs and effectively replace the now damaged and obsolete castles of Dyserth and Deganwy. That their building was meant to bring an imposed stability to the area is evident from the construction beside them of dependent town boroughs for English settlers. When the first war ended and terms were drawn up at Aberconwy, these northern cantrefs remained firmly under English rule and it was the two castles of Flint and Rhuddlan which ensured that they should continue to be so.

Building work here went ahead swiftly. By the end of August 1277 there were almost 2,300 diggers engaged on the new fortifications at Flint. This high number reflects both the sense of urgency and the great amount of earth-shifting involved in the castle's water defences, as well as protective earthworks for the town. Little damage was done here during the second Welsh campaign and, by 1284, the castle was mainly complete, at a cost of around £7,000.

Flint was built to an unusual plan. The normal four-square arrangement is offset, with one of the corner towers very much larger than the others and isolated from the enclosure. This Great Tower, or *Donjon*, is connected by drawbridge to the remainder of the castle and surrounded by its own water-filled moat. The entire castle was originally encircled by water, fed from the estuary of the river Dee, so that it was fully accessible by ship. To the

(continued on page 29)

Cestyll Edward I yng Nghymru

CRYNODEB

Rhwng 1277 a 1295, o ganlyniad i'w ddwy ymgyrch filwrol yng Nghymru, cododd y Brenin Edward I gyfres o gestyll mawrion yma. Yn ystod teyrnasiad ei ragflaenydd, y Brenin Henry III, yr oedd Llywelyn ap Gruffydd, tywysog Gogledd Cymru, wedi ennill goruchafiaeth lwyr dros y rhannau o'r wlad a oedd yn dal yn annibynnol; ond pan fu farw Henry, gwrthododd gydnabod goruchafiaeth y brenin newydd, Edward I, ac yn y diwedd aeth brenin Lloegr i ryfel oherwydd yr anghydfod.

Ar ôl ymgyrch fer yn ystod haf 1277 darostyngwyd Llywelyn a daeth y Sais i reoli rhannau helaeth o ganolbarth a gogledd-ddwyrain y wlad. Codwyd pedwar castell pwysig – Aberystwyth, Llanfair-ym-Muallt, y Fflint a Rhuddlan – o ganlyniad i'r frwydr hon a rhannwyd tiroedd Cymru ar orchymyn Lloegr.

Ym 1282 gwrthryfelodd y Cymry, o dan arweiniad brawd anfodlon Llywelyn, sef Dafydd. Lladdwyd Llywelyn ei hun ym mis Rhagfyr y flwyddyn honno, ac erbyn y mis Mehefin dilynol roedd y cyfan ar ben. Y tro hwn, bwriedid i fuddugoliaeth y Sais fod yn derfynol. Cychwynnodd y Brenin Edward ar gyfres o amddiffynfeydd anferth ar hyd yr arfordir, er mwyn amgylchynu amddiffynfa fynyddig y Cymry yn Eryri. Atgyfnerthid y rhain – yng Nghonwy, Caernarfon, Harlech a hen gastell Cymreig Cricieth – gan geyrydd yn y berfeddwlad yn hen gestyll Cymreig Dolwyddelan, Castell y Bere a Chaergwrle a oedd wedi eu hatgyweirio; at hyn, perswadiodd y brenin ei arglwyddi ar y Gororau i godi eu cestyll eu hunain yn Ninbych, Holt a'r Waun. Gyda'i gilydd, yr oedd cyfanswm cost adeiladau'r brenin tua £80,000 (tua £48 miliwn yn arian heddiw), ond roedd hynny'n llai nag a wariwyd gan y brenin ar y ddau ryfel yma.

Defnyddiwyd gweithwyr dan orfodaeth, o bob rhan o Loegr, i godi'r cestyll anferth hyn yng Ngogledd Cymru: cyflogwyd tua 3,000 ohonynt, ac mae manylion am eu tâl ar glawr a chadw. Y person a oedd yn gyffredinol gyfrifol am y gwaith adeiladu oedd pensaer Ffrengig o Savoy, y Meistr James o St George, ac nid rhyfedd felly fod tebygrwydd pendant ym manylion y cestyll hyn a chestyll Savoy. Cwblhawyd y mwyafrif ymhen pump i saith mlynedd, a'u hadeiladu'n enghraifft gampus o drefnu dynion a defnyddiau. Yn eu hamddiffynfeydd defnyddient dechnegau diweddaraf y dydd – muriau o fewn muriau, tai porth mawr, grymus a rhodfeydd mur ar lawer lefel. Gyda bron pob un yr oedd bwrdeistref lle'r anogid masnachwyr Seisnig i ymsefydlu ac felly helpu newid patrwm byw y wlad. Roedd y trefi hyn yn wreiddiol ar gau i'r Cymry, ond wedyn fe'u hagorwyd i bawb ac yn y diwedd daethant mor Gymreig ag unrhyw drefi eraill.

CASTELL Y FFLINT

Y Fflint oedd castell cyntaf ymgyrch 1277, ac ar y cyd â Rhuddlan fe'i bwriadwyd i ddod â rheolaeth barhaol dros yr ardal i'r dwyrain o Afon Clwyd, ardal a fuasai'n destun dadl ers cryn amser. Yn ystod ei dymor cyntaf cyflogwyd bron 2,300 o gloddwyr yma i weithio ar amddiffynfeydd y dref a ffosydd dŵr y castell: erbyn 1284 yr oedd wedi ei gwblhau bron, am gost derfynol o ryw £7,000 (tua £4m heddiw).

Codwyd castell y Fflint ar gynllun anarferol, ac yn ei batrwm sgwâr ceir y Tŵr Mawr, crwn a oedd yn fwy na'r tri arall ac ychydig o'r neilltu ac iddo 'i amddiffynfa ei hun. Yr oedd yn hawdd cyrraedd y castell o'r môr, ac yn wreiddiol amgylchynid ef gan ddŵr. Yn y Tŵr Mawr, sy'n debyg iawn i hwnnw yn Yverdon, Savoy, ceid grŵp o ystafelloedd preifat ar gyfer naill ai cwnstabl y castell neu brifustus Caer pan fyddai'n cynnal llys yn y Fflint. Ychydig hanes diweddarach sydd i'r castell, ond ymddengys yn *Richard II* gan Shakespeare fel safle gorchfygiad olaf y brenin hwnnw.

CASTELL RHUDDLAN

Saif Rhuddlan ar fan croesi isaf Afon Clwyd a gwelwyd ymsefydlu yno ers amser maith. Blaenoriaeth gyntaf y Brenin Edward ym 1277 oedd ei gwneud yn bosibl i longau'r môr ddefnyddio'r afon drwy gloddio sianel ddofn newydd. Ar ôl tair blynedd a gwario £800 roedd wedi ei chwblhau, a dyma wely'r afon hyd heddiw.

Consentrig yw'r castell gan fod iddo ddwy linell o amddiffynfeydd, ac ymestynnai'r ward allanol ar un ochr i lawr at yr afon, lle'r oedd doc a amddiffynnid ar gyfer llongau. Mae'r ward mewnol ar ffurf diamwnt ac yn gymesurol â dau dŷ porth mawr, a grŵp o adeiladau o'i fewn yn cynnwys ystafelloedd preifat ar gyfer y brenin a'r frenhines.

Ym mis Mawrth 1284 cyhoeddwyd Statud Rhuddlan yn diffinio'r cyfreithiau y bwriadai'r Brenin Edward eu defnyddio i reoli Cymru. Yma'n fuan wedyn, yn ôl traddodiad, cyflwynodd y brenin ei fab ifanc, yng ngŵydd arweinwyr y Cymry, fel eu tywysog newydd, un na allai siarad Saesneg ac a aned yng Nghymru.

CASTELL CONWY

Wrth y groesfan ar aber yr afon ac i ddiogelu'r ffordd trwy gefn gwlad i Eryri, saif Castell Conwy ar safle amddiffynnol naturiol. Yma eisoes ym 1284 safai abaty Sistersaidd Aberconwy, ac i gychwyn roedd yn rhaid i'r brenin gael safle newydd ar gyfer hwn, ymhellach i fyny'r afon.

Erbyn 1287 yr oedd amddiffynfeydd Conwy wedi eu cwblhau, ac wedi costio £14,000 (£8½m yn arian heddiw). Rhennir y castell yn ddau ward, y naill yn annibynnol ar y llall, a cheir amddiffynfeydd barbicaidd yn y naill ben a'r llall. Yn y ward allanol ceid adeiladau domestig a neuadd fawr, ac yn y ward mewnol grŵp o ystafelloedd preifat ar gyfer y brenin a'r frenhines. Gall Conwy ymfalchïo yn y muriau tref amddiffynnol gorau yng Ngogledd Cymru: mae dros ¾ milltir (1¼ km) ohonynt yn amgáu'r hen dref yn llwyr, a safent yn wreiddiol 30 tr (9m) o uchder, wedi'u gwyngalchu fel y castell.

Gorfodwyd y Brenin Edward I i lochesu am gyfnod yng Nghastell Conwy yn ystod gwrthryfel Madog ym 1295, ond daliodd y muriau'n gadarn. Gan na ddefnyddiwyd y lle byth wedyn ar gyfer unrhyw amddiffyn o ddifri, fe'i gadawyd i ddadfeilio.

CASTELL HARLECH

Ar yr olwg gyntaf, Harlech yw'r mwyaf syfrdanol o holl gestyll Edward I yng Ngogledd Cymru, gan ei fod yn sefyll ar safle creigiog urddasol yn edrych allan dros y môr. Erbyn 1289 yr oedd y castell mawr, consentrig hwn wedi ei gwblhau. Yr oedd ward mewnol petryal gyda thŵr ym mhob cornel iddo a thŷ porth anferth ar draws ei lenfur dwyreiniol. Yn hwnnw roedd grŵp o ystafelloedd preifat ar gyfer cwnstabl y castell. O'r ward allanol, disgynnai grisiau cerrig wedi'u hamddiffyn i lawr ar hyd y graig at y môr a'r llongau. Y pryd hwnnw hwyliai llongau'n agos iawn at y castell cyn i'r môr gilio.

Ym 1294, gwrthsafodd Harlech ymosodiadau Madog ap Gruffydd gan iddo gael ei gyflenwi â bwyd ar draws y môr, o Iwerddon. Ym 1404 syrthiodd i Owain Glyndŵr, a bu'n bencadlys iddo am bum mlynedd cyn ei ail-gipio yn y diwedd. Drigain mlynedd yn ddiweddarach, yn ystod Rhyfeloedd y Rhosynnau, daliwyd Harlech gan gefnogwyr teulu Lancaster mewn gwrthsafiad dewr a roes fod i'r gân *Gwŷr Harlech.*

CASTELL CAERNARFON

Yr oedd chwedlau wedi tyfu o gwmpas Caernarfon ymhell cyn i Edward I sefydlu ei gastell yma ym 1283. Mae'n debyg mai ei chaer Rufeinig, Segontium, a ysbrydolodd chwedl Macsen Wledig yn y *Mabinogion,* ac ymddengys i'r Brenin Edward wneud ymdrech fwriadol i ymgorffori elfennau o'r chwedl honno yn ei greadigaeth bensaernïol newydd.

Mae tyrau amlochrog i gastell Caernarfon ac ar y tu allan ceir haenau o garreg liw sy'n rhoi golwg wirioneddol urddasol iddo. O ran cynllun mae ar ffurf awrwydr wedi'i rannu, yn ei fan culaf, yn ddau ward. O fewn ei linell sengl o lenfuriau mae llu o amddiffynfeydd : mae i'r porth cadarn, Porth y Brenin, bum drws a chwe phorthcwlis, ac o fewn ei lenfuriau ceir rhodfeydd mur ar ddwy lefel.

Ar ôl ei ddifrodi yng ngwrthryfel Madog ym 1294, gwrthsafodd ymosodiadau gan Owain Glyndŵr ac nid ildiwyd y lle wedyn tan y Rhyfel Cartref. Fe'i hadferwyd yn helaeth yn ystod y ganrif ddiwethaf, ac yn fwy diweddar cynhaliwyd yma seremonïau arwisgo dau Dywysog Cymru.

CASTELL BIWMARES

Yn wahanol i bob un o gestyll eraill y Brenin Edward I yng Ngogledd Cymru, codwyd Castell Biwmares nid ar ôl yr un o'r ddau ryfel yn erbyn y Cymry, ond o ganlyniad i wrthryfel o dan arweiniad Madog ap Llywelyn ym 1294-95. Fe'i codwyd ar dir corsiog gwastad i reoli croesfan yr hen fferi i'r tir mawr. Biwmares yw'r pegwn eithaf mewn cynllunio cestyll consentrig - wedi'i osod yn gymesur ac yn anodd ei oresgyn drwy ymosodiad neu drwy lwgu'r trigolion hyd at ildio. O gwmpas y castell mae ffos ddŵr ac yr oedd iddo ddoc a ddiogelid ar gyfer llongau. Amddiffynnir y ward allanol gan fur allanol isel ag iddo un ar bymtheg o dyrau, ac yn y ward mewnol anferth ceir dau dŷ porth mawr a chwe thŵr ychwangeol i'w ddiogelu.

Oherwydd ymrwymiadau'r brenin mewn mannau eraill, ni chwblhawyd y castell erioed ac mae'r olwg bwt sydd arno yn adlewyrchu hynny, oherwydd ni chodwyd yr un o'r tyrau mewnol i'w lawn uchder. Ar ôl bywyd stormus, ildiwyd Biwmares yn y diwedd i'r Senedd yn y rhyfel Catref, a'r un fu stori pob un o'r cestyll yng Nghymru yn y pen draw.

Les Châteaux du Roi Edouard Ier au Pays de Galles

RESUME

Entre 1277 et 1295, le roi Edouard Ier acheva la construction d'une série de puissants châteaux-forts au Pays de Galles par suite des deux campagnes militaires qu'il y mena. Durant le règne de son prédécesseur, le roi Henri III, Llywelyn ap Gruffydd, prince du Nord du Pays de Galles, s'était assuré une supériorité totale sur les régions du pays encore indépendantes. A la mort d'Henri III, il se refusa à reconnaître la suzeraineté du nouveau roi, Edouard Ier. Ce différend devait finalement amener le roi d'Angleterre à lui déclarer la guerre.

A l'issue d'une brève campagne pendant l'été de 1277, Llywelyn fut vaincu et les Anglais s'emparèrent du contrôle de régions s'étendant au centre et au nord-est du Pays de Galles. Quatre châteaux-forts importants - ceux d'Aberystwyth, de Builth, de Flint et de Rhuddlan - furent construits par suite de cette expédition et les terres du Pays de Galles furent divisées par décret anglais.

En 1282, les Gallois se soulevèrent sous la conduite du frère dissident de Llywelyn, Dafydd. Llywelyn fut lui-même tué en décembre de cette même année et, au mois de juin suivant, la révolte était matée. Cette fois-ci, les Anglais entendirent donner un caractère final à leur victoire. Le roi Edouard Ier entreprit de bâtir une ligne de fortifications côtières massives dont l'objet était d'encercler la place forte galloise des montagnes de Snowdonia. Ces nouveaux ouvrages, à Conwy, Caernarfon, Harlech ainsi que l'ancien château gallois de Criccieth, étaient renforcés par des fortifications, à l'intérieur du pays, aménagées dans les châteaux gallois de Dolwyddelan, Castell y Bere et Hope, qui avaient subi des réparations. Le roi persuada également les seigneurs de la marche à se construire des châteaux à Denbigh, Holt et Chirk. Le coût total de ces travaux de construction royale devait se monter à environ £80.000 (quelque £48 m d'aujourd'hui), un montant toutefois inférieur à celui que le roi avait consacré à deux campagnes au Pays de Galles.

Pour construire ces puissants ouvrages dans le nord du Pays de Galles, il fallut faire appel à une main-d'oeuvre embauchée de force dans toutes les régions de l'Angleterre. Environ trois mille ouvriers furent engagés et la comptabilité de leur rémunération est en grande partie conservée. Un architecte savoyard, Maître Jacques de Saint George, fut chargé de superviser les travaux, et il n'est pas surprenant de constater des similarités de détails entre ces châteaux et ceux de Savoie. La plupart d'entre eux furent achevés en l'espace de cinq à sept ans et leur construction témoigne d'une belle gestion des hommes et des matériaux. Les défenses mises en place dans ces châteaux firent appel aux techniques les plus avancées de l'époque – des murs doublés par d'autres murs, d'énormes corps-de-garde et des passages à plusieurs niveaux dans les remparts. Ces châteaux étaient presque tous entourés de bourgades où les marchands anglais étaient encouragés à venir s'installer afin d'aider à changer les moeurs des indigènes. Fermés à l'origine aux Gallois, ces bourgades furent par la suite ouvertes à tous, et finirent par devenir entièrement galloises.

LE CHATEAU DE FLINT

Flint fut le premier château issu de la campagne de 1277. Comme celui de Rhuddlan, il avait pour but d'imposer le contrôle anglais sur une région longtemps contestée à l'est de la rivière Clwyd. Au cours de la première saison des travaux, près de deux mille trois cents ouvriers furent affectés aux travaux de terrassement de la ville et des défenses d'eau du château. Ces travaux étaient presque achevés en 1284 pour une dépense finale d'environ £7.000 (ce qui représente £4 m en monnaie d'aujourd'hui).

Adoptant un plan inhabituel, la disposition carrée du château de Flint se signale par une tour ronde décentrée, qui est plus grande que les trois autres et défendue séparément. On pouvait accéder directement au château par la mer et celui-ci était à l'origine entouré d'eau.

Sa Grande Tour, qui ressemble fortement à celle du château d'Yverdon, en Savoie (maintenant Vaud CH) comportait une suite de pièces privées à l'usage du gouverneur du château ou du justicier de Chester, lorsque celui-ci tenait sa cour à Flint. Le château ne connut guère, par la suite, d'événements historiques, mais figura dans la tragédie *Richard II* de Shakespeare comme lieu de la défaite finale du roi.

LE CHATEAU DE RHUDDLAN

Le château se trouve au passage à gué de la rivière Clwyd le plus en aval, et sert depuis longtemps de lieu d'établissement. La première priorité du roi Edouard Ier en 1277 était de rendre la rivière navigable aux bâtiments de mer en creusant un nouveau chenal à eau profonde. Cet ouvrage fut achevé trois ans plus tard au coût de £800 et supporte aujourd'hui le cours du fleuve.

Le château est un ouvrage concentrique entouré de deux enceintes défensives parallèles. L'enclos extérieur se prolongeait d'un côté jusqu'au fleuve où un quai protégé était aménagé pour la navigation. L'enclos intérieur épouse la forme symétrique d'un losange. Il est pourvu de deux énormes corps de garde et contient des appartements pour le roi et la reine. C'est ici que fut proclamé, en 1284, le Grand Statut du Pays de Galles, définissant les lois aux termes desquelles le roi Edouard Ier entendait gouverner ce pays. Peu après, si l'on en croit tradition postérieure, le roi présenta son fils enfant aux chefs gallois comme leur nouveau prince, né au pays de Galles et ne parlant pas anglais.

LE CHATEAU DE CONWY

Le château de Conwy se trouve sur un site de défense naturel, protégeant la route terrestre menant vers le massif de Snowdonia au croisement avec l'estuaire de la rivière.

L'abbaye cistercienne d'Aberconwy se trouvait déjà à cet emplacement en 1284 et le roi eut à lui trouver un nouveau site plus en amont.

En 1287, les fortifications du château de Conwy étaient achevées. Elles avaient côuté environ £14.000 (quelque £8½ m en monnaie d'aujourd'hui). Le château est divisé en deux secteurs, indépendants l'un de l'autre et dotés de barbacanes à chaque extrémité. Le secteur extérieur abritait les bâtiments domestiques et une grande salle. Le secteur intérieur comportait les appartements privés du roi et de la reine. Conwy se targue du plus bel ensemble de remparts de cité fortifiée du nord du Pays de Galles. Ces remparts entourent complètement la vieille ville sur plus d'1¼ kilomètre. Ils s'élevaient à l'origine à 9 mètres de hauteur et étaient blanchis à la chaux comme le château.

Le roi Edouard Ier fut obligé de se réfugier quelque temps au château de Conwy pendant le soulèvement Madog en 1295, mais les murs tinrent bon. Plus jamais sollicitée par des assauts sérieux, cette place forte fut progressivement abandonnée au déclin.

LE CHATEAU DE HARLECH

Le château de Harlech est d'emblée l'ouvrage le plus frappant construit par Edouard Ier dans le nord du Pays de Galles, se dressant comme il le fait sur un piton rocheux dominant la mer. Ce grand château concentrique fut achevé en 1289: il était doté d'un enclos intérieur rectangulaire avec quatre tours d'angle. Il comportait un énorme corps-de-garde construit à cheval sur la courtine est et dans lequel avait été aménagée une suite d'appartements privés pour le gouverneur du château. Un escalier de pierre protégé descendait de l'enclos extérieur, à même le rocher, donnant accès à la mer et à la navigation qui pouvait, à cette époque, gagner le château, la mer n'ayant pas reculé à sa position actuelle.

En 1294, le château de Harlech résista aux assauts de Madog, étant approvisionné par la mer à partir de l'Irlande. En 1404, il tomba aux mains d'Owain Glyndŵr dont il demeura le quartier général pendant cinq ans avant d'être finalement repris. Soixante ans plus tard, pendant la Guerre des Roses, Harlech fut tenu par le camp lancastrien au terme d'une résistance vaillante qui donna naissance à la chanson populaire *Men of Harlech.*

LE CHATEAU DE CAERNARFON

Caernarfon était entouré de légendes bien avant qu'Edouard Ier y fonda son château en 1283. Le fort romain de Segontium construit en cet endroit avait vraisemblablement inspiré la romance de Macsen Wledig dans le *Mabinogion*, et le roi Edouard chercha, semble-t-il, consciemment à incorporer des éléments de ce conte à sa nouvelle création architecturale.

Le château de Caernarfon est doté de tours polygonales et de stries extérieures en pierre colorée qui lui confèrent un aspect véritablement majestueux. Vu en plan, il a la forme d'un sablier et se divise en deux secteurs à son point le plus étroit. A l'intérieur de sa ligne unique de murs de courtine, il comporte de nombreux dispositifs défensifs – la Porte du Roi fortement défendue comporte cinq portes et six herses et ses murs de courtine sont pourvus de passages intérieurs continus à deux niveaux.

Après avoir été mis à sac lors de la rébellion de Madog en 1294, le château résista aux assauts d'Owain Glyndŵr et ne se rendit jamais jusqu'à la Guerre Civile. Largement restauré au cours du siècle dernier, il a plus récemment servi de cadre aux cérémonies d'investiture de deux Princes de Galles.

LE CHATEAU DE BEAUMARIS

A la différence des autres châteaux bâtis par le roi Edouard Ier dans le nord du Pays de Galles, celui de Beaumaris ne fut pas construit par suite des deux campagnes galloises, mais à l'issue d'une rébellion conduite par Madog ap Llywelyn en 1294-95. Construit sur un sol plat et marécageux en vue de dominer le site de l'ancienne liaison maritime vers la terre ferme, Beaumaris représente une conception ultime en matière de châteaux à structure concentrique. D'une disposition symétrique, il était particulièrement difficile à prendre d'assaut ou à soumettre par la faim. Il est entouré d'un fossé rempli d'eau et comportait un quai protégé pour la navigation. L'enclos extérieur est défendu par un mur bas extérieur comportant seize tours, tandis que le spacieux enclos intérieur est défendu par deux grands corps-de-garde et six tours supplémentaires.

Du fait des engagements du roi ailleurs, le château ne fut jamais achevé. Son aspect un peu trapu en témoigne, car aucune des tours intérieures ne fut construite à sa pleine hauteur. A l'issue d'une existence sans histoire, le château de Beaumaris fut finalement remis au Parlement lors de la Guerre Civile, tout comme le furent, pour finir, l'ensemble des châteaux de la Principauté de Galles.

König Edward I. und seine Burgen in Wales

ZUSAMMENFASSUNG

Zwischen 1277 und 1295 baute König Edward I. als Resultat seiner zwei Feldzüge in Wales eine großartige Reihe eindrucksvoller Burgen. Während der Regierungszeit seines Vorgängers, König Henry III., konnte Llywelyn ap Gruffydd, Prinz von Nordwales, die damals noch unabhängigen Regionen des Landes vollkommen in seine Macht bekommen. Nach dem Tode von Henry III. weigerte er sich jedoch, den neuen König Edward I. als seinen Overlord anzuerkennen. Dieser Streit führte schließlich dazu, daß der englische König den Krieg erklärte.

In einem kurzen Feldzug im Sommer 1277 wurde Llywelyn vollkommen unterworfen; die Engländer kontrollierten danach beträchtliche Bereiche im Zentrum und Nordosten des Landes. Vier bedeutende Befestigungsanlagen – Aberystwyth, Builth, Flint und Rhuddlan – wurden als Resultat dieser Kampagne gebaut. Die walisischen Ländereien wurden durch englisches Dekret aufgeteilt.

Es folgte im Jahre 1282 ein Aufstand der Waliser unter der Führung von Dafydd, dem feindlich gestimmten Bruder von Llywelyn. Llywelyn selbst fiel im Dezember dieses Jahres; im Juni des darauffolgenden Jahres war alles vorbei. Dieses Mal sollte sichergestellt werden, daß der englische Sieg auch für die Zukunft vollkommen war. König Edward begann mit dem Bau einer ganzen Serie massiver Küstenbefestigungen, die das Bollwerk der Waliser – Snowdonia – praktisch umzingelten. Diese neuen Bauten – in Conwy, Caernarfon, Harlech und der früheren walisischen Feste von Criccieth – wurden durch weitere Befestigungen im Land unterstützt, und zwar durch die wiederhergestellten walisischen Burgen von Dolwyddelan, Castell y Bere und Hope. Außerdem überredete der König seine Markgrafen, eigene Befestigungen zu bauen – und zwar in Denbigh, Holt und Chirk. Insgesamt beliefen sich die Kosten der königlichen Bauarbeiten auf etwa £80.000 (etwa £48 m nach heutigem Wert) – weniger als der König im Verlauf der zwei Kriege aufbringen mußte.

Zum Bau dieser mächtigen Burgen in Nordwales wurden Arbeitskräfte zwangsweise aus allen Teilen England eingezogen – etwa 3 000 Personen leisteten hier ihre Fronarbeit. Und viele Einzelheiten ihrer Bezahlung finden sich noch immer in den Dokumenten. Die Gesamtverantwortung für die Bauarbeiten lag bei einem französischen Architekten aus Savoy, Master James of St George.

Es ist daher nicht weiter überraschend, daß zwischen den hier gebauten Burgen und denen in Savoy erhebliche Ähnlichkeit besteht. Die meisten Festungen wurden innerhalb von 5 bis 7 Jahren fertiggestellt – ihr Bau war ein Triumph der Organisation von Arbeitskräften und Baumaterial. Die Befestigungsanlagen folgten den damals modernsten Erkenntnissen – ineinander verschachtelte Mauern, mächtige Wachtürme und Wandgänge auf vielen Ebenen. In der Nähe fast aller Burgen befanden sich sogenannte Burgflecken oder befestigte Ortschaften, in denen sich englische Kaufleute niederlassen konnten, um die Lebensart der ursprünglichen Bewohner zu verändern. Diese Ortschaften waren ursprünglich Walisern versperrt; als sie später ihre Tore öffneten, wurden sie genauso walisisch wie alle anderen Städte.

FLINT CASTLE

Die erste Burg der Kampagne von 1277 war Flint; zusammen mit Rhuddlan sollte diese Feste die lang umstrittene Region östlich vom Fluß Clwyd unter permanente Kontrolle bringen. Während der ersten Saison waren fast 2 300 Arbeitskräfte mit dem Graben der Wallbefestigungen für die Stadt und mit den Wassergräben der Burg beschäftigt. Im Jahre 1284 waren die

Bauarbeiten fast abgeschlossen; die Gesamtkosten beliefen sich auf etwa £7 000 (etwa £4 m nach heutigem Wert).

Der Grundriß von Flint ist etwas ungewöhnlich; die rechteckige Bauweise zeigt einen abgesetzten Rundturm, der eine separate Verteidigung ermöglichte und der größer als die anderen drei war. Die Burg war früher vollkommen von Wassergräben umgeben und vom Meer her zugänglich. Der Hauptturm, der dem von Yverdon in Savoy sehr ähnlich ist, umfaßte eine Reihe von Privaträumen, die entweder vom Burgkommandanten oder vom Justiziar von Chester bewohnt wurden, wenn dieser in Flint Gericht hielt. In der späteren Geschichte spielt die Burg kaum eine Rolle, obwohl sie in Shakespeares Richard II. als Schauplatz für die endgültige Niederlage dieses Königs verwendet wird.

RHUDDLAN CASTLE

Rhuddlan liegt an der niedrigsten Furtstelle des Flusses Clwyd, an einer Stelle, an der sich schon seit langem eine Ortschaft befindet. König Edward I. kam es im Jahre 1277 zunächst einmal darauf an, durch Ausbaggern des Flusses einen Kanal für seegängige Schiffe zu schaffen. Unter Aufwendung von etwa £800 konnte dieser Kanal, den der Fluß auch heute noch benutzt, drei Jahre später in Betrieb genommen werden.

Die Burg ist konzentrisch angelegt und besitzt zwei parallele Verteidigungslinien. Der äußere Burghof erstreckt sich auf einer Seite bis zum Fluß hinunter, wo sich ein befestigtes Dock für Schiffe befand. Der Innenhof ist rautenförmig und symmetrisch angelegt; er besitzt zwei wuchtige Torhäuser und Unterkunft mit Privaträumlichkeiten für den König und die Königin.

Im März 1284 wurde hier das Große Statut von Wales proklamiert, das die Gesetze enthielt, mit denen König Edward I. Wales regieren wollte. Der Tradition nach präsentierte hier König Edward I. wenig später den walisischen Fürsten seinen kleinen Sohn als den neuen Prinzen von Wales, der – wie versprochen – in Wales geboren war und kein Englisch sprach.

CONWY CASTLE

Conwy Castle liegt an der Übergangsstelle der Flußmündung und überwacht die Landroute nach Snowdonia in einer hervorragenden natürlichen Verteidigungsposition. Hier stand bereits im Jahre 1284 die Zisterzienzerabtei von Aberconwy; der König mußte zunächst einmal ein neues Gelände dafür etwas weiter flußaufwärts finden.

Die Befestigungen in Conwy waren 1287 abgeschlossen und kosteten etwa £14 000 (etwa £8½ m nach heutigem Wert). Die Burg läßt sich in zwei Hofbereiche aufteilen, die unabhängig voneinander sind. An den Enden sind jeweils Befestigungswerke vorgesehen. Auf dem äußeren Hof befanden sich Haushaltsgebäude und ein großer Saal, während der Innenhof eine Reihe von Privaträumlichkeiten für König und Königin umfaßte. Conwy zeigt die besterhaltenen Stadtbefestigungen in Nordwales. Mehr als 1¼ km umschließen vollkommen die Altstadt. Die Höhe der Mauern, die ursprüglich genauso wie die Burg getüncht waren, betrug 9 m.

Während der Madog-Revolte im Jahre 1295 mußte sich König Edward I. in Conwy Castle zurückziehen. Doch die Mauern hielten den Angriffen stand. Danach waren die Befestigungen keinerlei ernsten Attacken mehr ausgesetzt, so daß die Burg nach und nach verfiel.

HARLECH CASTLE

Harlech Castle ist sicher die imposanteste Burg aus der Zeit von Edward I. in Nordwales. Alleine schon der Standort sorgt dafür – hoch über dem Meer auf einem Felsen. Im Jahre 1289 war der Bau dieser großartigen, konzentrisch angelegten Burg abgeschlossen und umfaßte einen rechteckigen Innenhof mit einem Turm an jeder Ecke sowie ein wuchtiges Torhaus auf der östlichen Mantelmauer, wo eine Reihe von Privaträumen für den Burgkommandanten vorgesehen war. Vom Außenhof führte eine befestigte Steintreppe vom Felsen herab zum Meer, so daß Schiffe sehr nahe bis zur Burg segeln konnten, bevor das Meer auf den heutigen Küstenverlauf zurückging.

Im Jahre 1294 widerstand Harlech den Madog-Attacken und wurde von Irland aus zu Wasser verpflegt. Owain Glyndŵr eroberte die Burg im Jahre 1404 und benutzte sie fünf Jahre lang als Hauptquartier, bevor die Feste wieder in andere Hände fiel. Sechzig Jahre später wurde die Burg während der Rosenkriege von Lancaster-Truppen gehalten; ihr Widerstand wird in dem bekannten walisischen Nationallied "Men of Harlech" besungen.

CAERNARFON CASTLE

Caernarfon war schon immer von Sagen umwoben, lange bevor Edward I. hier seine Burg im Jahre 1283 baute. Das römische Festungswerk Segontium gab möglicherweise die Inspiration für eine Sammlung walisischer Erzählungen unter dem Titel Mabinogion (Macsen Wledig). König Edward schien sich bewußt darum zu bemühen, Elemente dieser Erzählungen in der neuen Feste miteinzubeziehen.

Die polygonalen Türme von Caernarfon besitzen außen Verzierungsstreifen aus farbigem Stein; ein wirklich majestätischer Anblick. Der Grundriß ist gewissermaßen sanduhrförmig und an der engsten Stelle in zwei Höfe aufgeteilt. Die einfache Mantelmauerverteidigung umschließt eine Vielzahl von Verteidigungswerken – das stark befestigte King's Gate besitzt fünf Tore und sechs Falltore. Die Mantelmauern sind mit durchgehenden Wandgängen auf zwei Ebenen versehen.

Nach einer Eroberung der Burg während der Madog-Revolte in 1294 widerstand die Feste jedoch den Angriffen von Owain Glyndŵr und konnte bis zum Bürgerkrieg immer gehalten werden. Die gesamte Anlage wurde im letzten Jahrhundert erheblich restauriert und diente seitdem zweimal als Veranstaltungsort für die Investitur des Prinzen von Wales.

BEAUMARIS CASTLE

Im Gegensatz zu allen anderen Burgen von König Edward I. in Nordwales wurde Beaumaris nicht nach den beiden walisischen Kriegen gebaut, sonder erst nach der Revolte von Madog ap Llywelyn 1294–95. Beaumaris steht auf ebenem Marschgelände und überwacht eine alte Fährenstelle zum Festland. Die Burg ist das vollendetste Beispiel einer konzentrischen, symmetrisch angelegten Bauweise – eines Bautyps, der nur schwer anzugreifen und kaum auszuhungern war. Umgeben wurde die Feste von einem Wassergraben, der unter anderem ein befestigtes Dock für Schiffe besaß. Die Verteidigung des Außenhofes erfolgte durch eine niedrige Außenmauer mit sechszehn Türmen, während der massive Innenhof zwei große Torhäuser sowie sechs weitere Türme zum Schutz der Anlage aufwies.

Aufgrund anderer Verpflichtungen war der König nicht in der Lage, den Bau dieser Burg zu vollenden. Sie sieht daher etwas niedrig geraten aus; keiner der Innentürme wurden je bis zur vollen Höhe konstruiert. Nach einer wenig ereignisreichen Geschichte wurde Beaumaris wie alle anderen Burgen in Wales während des Bürgerkriegs Parlamentstruppen übergeben.

south, a large outer bailey, standing between the castle and town, was approached by a stone causeway. Within the inner bailey there were domestic buildings, which have now entirely disappeared; no doubt, these would have included a hall, chapel and kitchen, together with a bakehouse, brewhouse and so on.

No other castle built by Edward I has a plan comparable to that of Flint. The closest parallel and the most likely inspiration for its design is to be found in the castle of Yverdon, in Savoy, where Master James of St George had been employed in the 1260s. Here, too, a rectangular enclosure is accompanied by a larger offset round tower and it bears a striking resemblance to that at Flint. There are no records for the use made of Flint's Great Tower; its central chamber is encircled by a continuous outer passageway, which was divided into rooms and contained a chapel, together with a well. The basement was probably used for the storage of items such as clothing, ammunition, arms and armour, while the upper floor, or floors, would have provided accommodation either for the castle's constable, or as a judge's lodging for use by the justiciar of Chester when holding court in Flint.

There is an account for the making of a timber gallery to enclose the top of the great tower, but how this might have looked we cannot tell, for all evidence has disappeared together with the vanished upper storey.

In later history, the castle is best known for its role in the downfall of King Richard II. Lured from the safety of Conwy Castle, in August 1399, the luckless king was ambushed on the road and escorted to Flint, there to await the coming of his arch-rival, Henry Bolingbroke, Duke of Lancaster. From Flint, Richard was taken to London and forced to sign a deed of abdication, while Bolingbroke became King Henry IV in his stead.

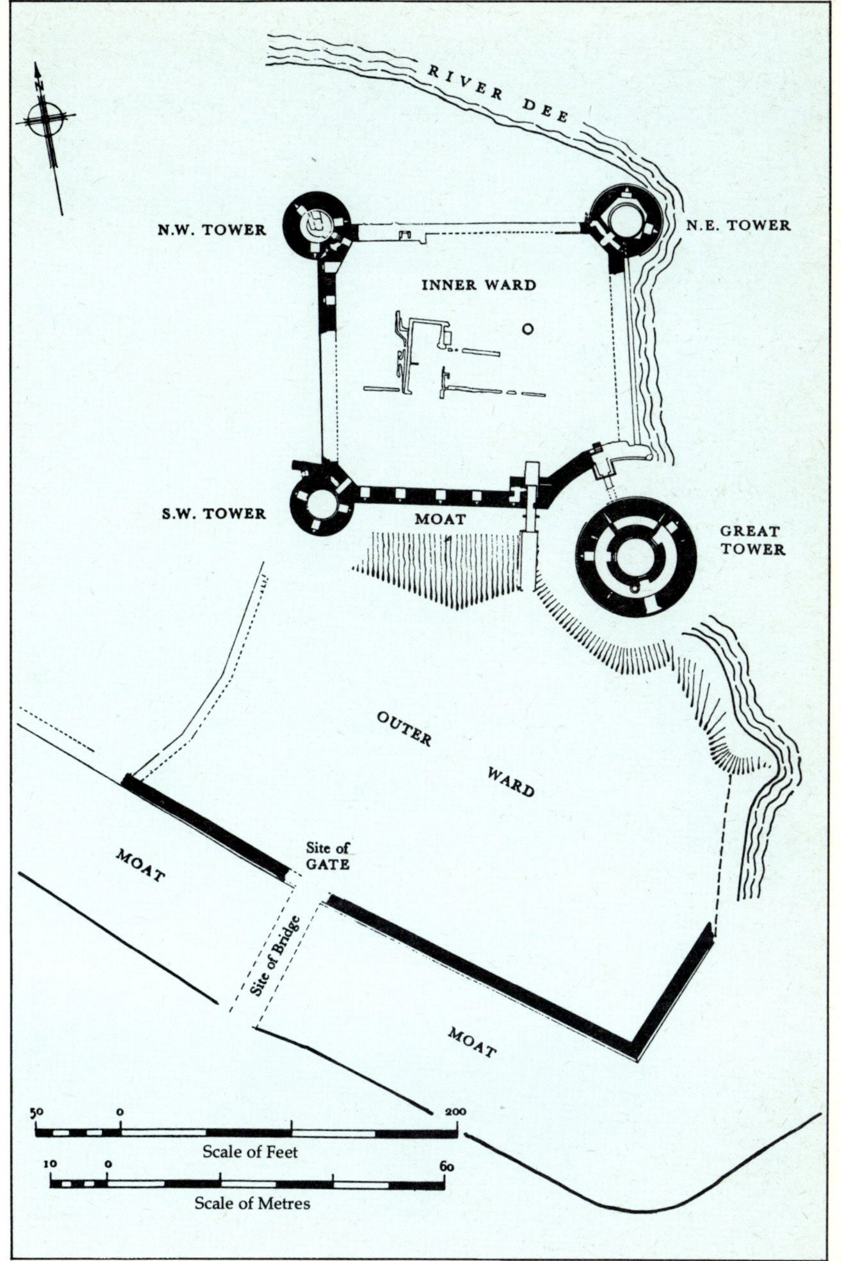

37 *Flint Castle*
37 *Castell y Fflint*
37 *Le Château de Flint*
37 *Flint Castle*

Rhuddlan
Castle

Situated at the lowest fording of the river Clwyd, Rhuddlan has long been a place of settlement. It lies at the heart of an area which was continually changing hands between Wales and England. Gruffydd ap Llywelyn, Prince of Gwynedd, founded a palace here in 1063. Ten years later, Gruffydd's palace was destroyed and replaced by Robert of Rhuddlan's Norman earthwork motte and bailey castle, which can still be seen beside the river a short distance away from its Edwardian successor.

When, in the summer of 1277, King Edward I decided to build at Rhuddlan a replacement to the former hill castle of Dyserth, the first necessity was to make the river Clwyd navigable to sea-going shipping. This required the excavation of a new channel to replace the old meandering river bed over a two to three mile (3·2 km – 4·8 km) distance to the sea. It was a formidable task, involving considerable allocation of labour and expenditure and it took three years and nearly £800 to complete. Despite the obvious difficulties, however, the work has stood the test of time insofar as the river course today is, by and large, that to which King Edward diverted it more than 700 years ago.

Rhuddlan is the first of the English royal castles at which Master James of St George is recorded in charge of the operations and certain features of the building, such as the positioning of latrine shafts and the diagonal inner angle of its corner towers, are recognisable Savoyard techniques. In its planning, the castle is concentric, having two parallel lines of defence. The outer ward is surrounded, on three sides, by a dry moat; on the fourth, it extended down to the river, where there was a protected dock

39

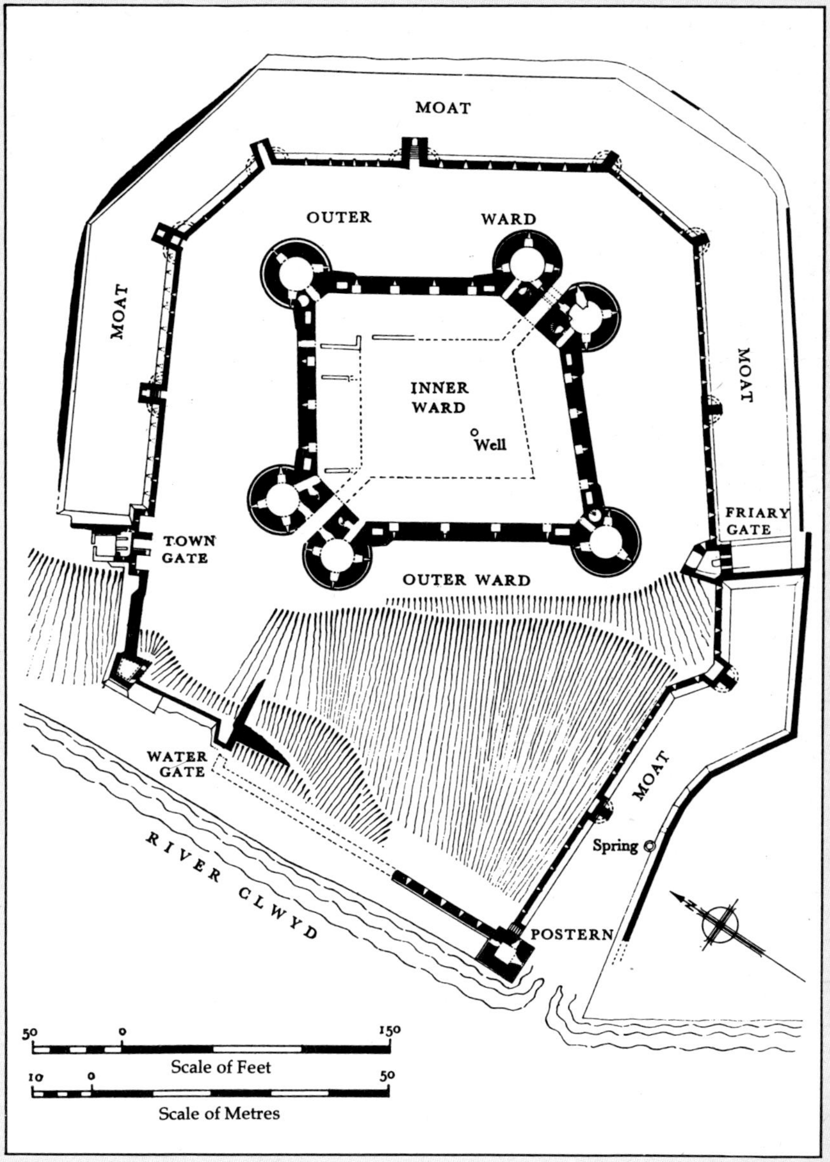

39 *Rhuddlan Castle*
39 *Castell Rhuddlan*
39 *Le Château de Rhuddlan*
39 *Rhuddlan Castle*

38 *View from across the river*
38 *Golygfa ar draws yr afon*
38 *Vue de la rivière en largeur*
38 *Ansicht vom Fluß aus*

38

40 *Reconstruction drawing by Alan Sorrell*
40 *Darlun, ailgynhyrchiad gan Alan Sorrell*
40 *Plan de reconstruction par Alan Sorrell*
40 *Rekonstruktionszeichnung von Alan Sorrell*

41 *The west gatehouse*
41 *Tŷ porth y gorllewin*
41 *Corps-de-garde Ouest*
41 *Westl. Torhaus*

for shipping. Four gates – two from the river, two from the town – led into the outer ward, while guarding the massively built inner ward there are two great twin-towered gatehouses. The inner ward itself is diamond shaped and symmetrical in layout; accommodation within it included a suite of royal apartments and, between 1283 and 1286, large sums were spent here on private rooms and a chapel for Queen Eleanor. Most of these inner buildings would have been timber-framed structures, placed against the curtain walls, but only slight foundations and roof traces remain today to show where they once stood.

The town, which adjoined the castle, had an enclosing bank and ditch on three sides, crowned by a wooden palisade; on the fourth side, adequate defence was provided by the steep river bank. Edward's new borough was built to the west of the old Norman settlement and was approached, across the new deep-water channel, by an opening timber bridge. It was laid out to a typical grid pattern – still followed by its streets today – and was granted its first charter in November 1278. King Edward evidently took great pride in his civic foundation for, in 1281, he applied to Rome for permission to replace the nearby cathedral of St Asaph by a new structure at Rhuddlan. He seems to have been quite prepared to expend a good deal of money and labour on the project, but all eventually came to nought.

Rhuddlan's place in history is assured by the issuing there, in March 1284, of the Great Statute of Wales (*see page 9*)—a settlement for the country which lasted until Wales was merged with England at the Act of Union, in 1536. Also, according to a tradition of 300 years later, the king is supposed to have named or presented his infant son, born at Caernarfon that April, to the assembled Welsh leaders at Rhuddlan just a few months later, telling them that here was their new prince Edward, who was *borne in Wales and could speake never a word of English, whose life and conversation no man was able to staine.*

42 *View from the air*
42 *Golygfa o'r awyr*
42 *Vue aérienne*
42 *Ansicht von oben*

42

Conwy Castle

43

Edward I gained control of the Conwy valley in March 1283, during his second campaign in Wales. Almost immediately he began work on a new fortress to secure the estuary crossing and replace the older castle of Deganwy, on the opposite side. The site chosen was a natural one for defence, washed on three sides by the waters of the Conwy river and its tributary, the Gyffin: it had the advantages of a ready supply of building stone and accessibility by ship and it fitted well into a developing pattern of fortifications designed to secure the north Wales coast route. Close by, on the site of the future town, there already stood a former residence of Llywelyn ap Gruffydd and also the buildings of the Cistercian abbey of Aberconwy. Although this entailed the king having to provide for the re-establishment of the abbey elsewhere, the accommodation thus available was yet a further inducement towards the founding of a castle here, for the existing buildings could be pressed into service by the occupying forces almost immediately.

Priority was first given to the building of timber-framed apartments for the king and queen, near to the abbey in the town. By July, the queen's lodgings

43 *View from the town walls*
43 *Golygfa o furiau'r dref*
43 *Vue depuis les murs de la ville*
43 *Ansicht von der Stadtmauer*

44

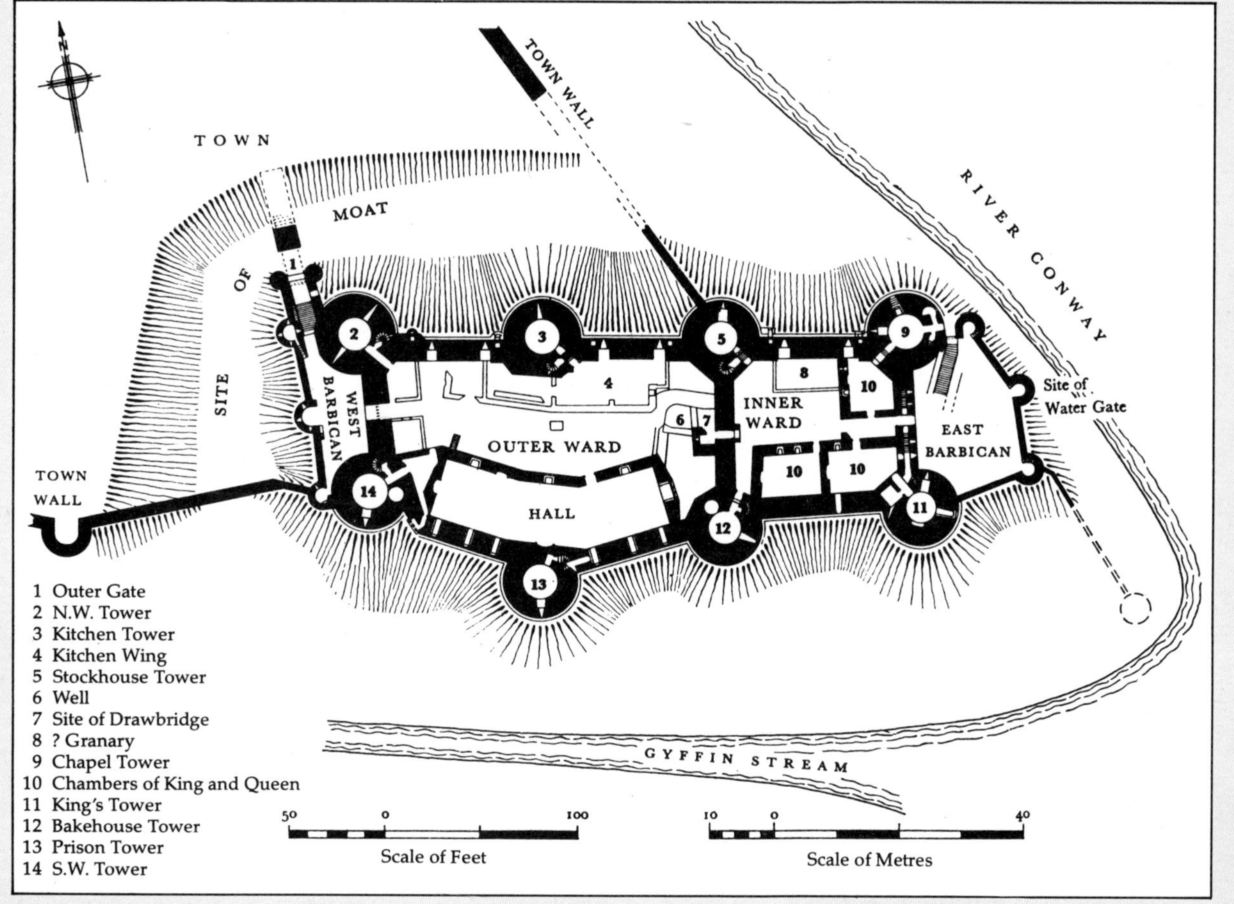

44 *Conwy Castle*
44 *Castell Conwy*
44 *Le Château de Conwy*
44 *Conwy Castle*

were completed; outside them was a garden—its turf shipped specially from further up river—and 3d was paid to one of her squires, Roger le Fykeys, for attending to its first watering. Seven miles (11.2 km) up the Conwy, at Maenan, new buildings were erected for the displaced Cistercian abbey and, in October 1284, these were dedicated and complete. The former abbey church was retained to serve as the parish church for the new town, as indeed it does still.

The main task in hand, however, was the building of the castle and town. Of all the construction works then underway, the main effort was directed here and, within two seasons, almost £6,000 had been spent. Originally, it seems, Conwy, and not Caernarfon, was proposed as the main shire town – it was certainly by far the largest of the north Wales boroughs, having a circuit of more than ¾ mile (1 km) of town walls 30 ft (9 m) high, with 22 towers and three gateways.

By the end of 1287, after an expenditure of more than £14,000, the new fortifications stood virtually complete. The castle, on its narrow spur of rock, has a linear plan, with four pairs of great round towers and lower barbican defences at each end. It is divided by a cross wall into two wards, either of which could hold out if the other fell. The outer ward, approached from within the town by way of an enormous ramp and drawbridge, contained domestic buildings (now merely foundations) and a great hall of noble proportions, whose decorated windows were no doubt once emblazoned with stained glass. At the east end, the only external

45 *Imaginative scene in the Great Hall by Alan Sorrell*
45 *Golygfa ddychmygol yn y Neuadd Fawr gan Alan Sorrell*
45 *Scène imaginaire dans la Grande Salle par Alan Sorrell*
45 *Mögliche Szene im Rittersaal (Great Hall); Zeichnung: Alan Sorrell*

46 *Reconstruction drawing by Alan Sorrell*
46 *Darlun, ailgynhyrchiad gan Alan Sorrell*
46 *Plan de reconstruction par Alan Sorrell*
46 *Rekonstruktionszeichnung von Alan Sorrell*

approach to the square inner ward was by water, for added security; here lay an entire suite of stone-built royal apartments, protected safe within its turretted battlements and, in the north-eastern tower, a small chapel, which still displays a quality of decoration unmatched at any other Edwardian castle. Both castle and town walls were originally rendered and whitened – a very common treatment for most major buildings in the middle ages. In the sunlight, they must have presented a gleaming spectacle crowned, as they were, by the groups of pinnacles that are such a feature of Conwy's battlements still.

In January 1295, during the Madog uprising, King Edward I was forced to take refuge in Conwy Castle; food and drink ran dangerously low before help arrived, but the walls stood firm. The greatest battle that the castle had to face, however, was the one against decay. From only a generation after its completion, there are constant references to the repair and re-roofing of this or that part of the building. The changed political climate under the Tudors must have lessened the need for such renewals and, by 1627, the castle was so far decayed as to be dangerous to enter. Defended briefly in the Civil War, it was surrendered to Parliament in 1646 and was subsequently gutted and left to the mercies of wind and weather.

47

47 *The Castle and walled town from the air*
47 *Y Castell, y dref a'i muriau o'r awyr*
47 *Vue aérienne du château et des murs d'enceinte de la ville*
47 *Burg und Stadtbefestigungen (Ansicht von oben)*

Harlech Castle

Of all the castles built by King Edward I in north Wales, Harlech's situation is the most spectacular. Perfectly adapted to the restricted, rocky crag, the building possesses beauty of line, an aura of power and a position of great natural strength.

Just as the capture of the Welsh castle of Dolwyddelan, had cleared the way for an advance down the Conwy valley and the founding of a castle there, in March 1283, so the taking of Castell y Bere, a month later, enabled the English army to march up through Meirionnydd and make a base at Harlech. Preparations for a new castle here began almost at once, under the superintendence of Master James of St George who, by this time, must have been finding it increasingly difficult to oversee all the jobs now in hand. Construction at Harlech, however, progressed steadily from inception to completion within seven years. Although few details are known to us of the work in its first three seasons, up to 950 men are recorded as employed on the castle from 1286 onwards. Labour here, as elsewhere, was paid for on a piecework basis and, among other such payments, a certain Master William of Drogheda received £117, in 1289, for building the south tower toward the sea 52 ft (15.8 m) high at a rate of 45 shillings per foot.

By the end of 1289, the great concentric castle stood virtually complete. The rectangular inner ward has a tower at each corner and, on three sides, there are now only foundations of the buildings once ranged around its walls – two halls and their associated service areas, a chapel and the castle well. The main private accommodation lay within its three-storey gatehouse, which stands centrally astride the eastern curtain. Above the ground level guard-chambers were two self-contained suites of rooms, one for visiting dignitaries and the other for the constable, or governor of the castle who, in 1290 and for three years following, was none other than Master James of St George. Apart from the gatehouse, Harlech's other remarkable feature is the defended 'Way from the Sea', an enclosed stairway which plunged almost 200 ft (60 m) down to the base of the castle rock, where a lower gate gave access to shipping. At that time, vessels could sail close in but, today, the sea has receded over half a mile (0.8 km) away, leaving the castle isolated upon its rock.

Harlech played a far more prominent role in history than did any other Welsh castle of Edward I. Its first testing came in 1294 when, although cut off to landward, it was supplied and victualled by sea from Ireland and so withstood the assaults of the rebels under Madog. In the great national uprising, led by Owain Glyndŵr, both Harlech and Aberystwyth Castles were taken in 1404, after long sieges. Harlech then became the headquarters of

48 *View from the air*
48 *Golygfa o'r awyr*
48 *Vue aérienne*
48 *Ansicht von oben*

49 *Harlech Castle*
49 *Castell Harlech*
49 *Le Château de Harlech*
49 *Harlech Castle*

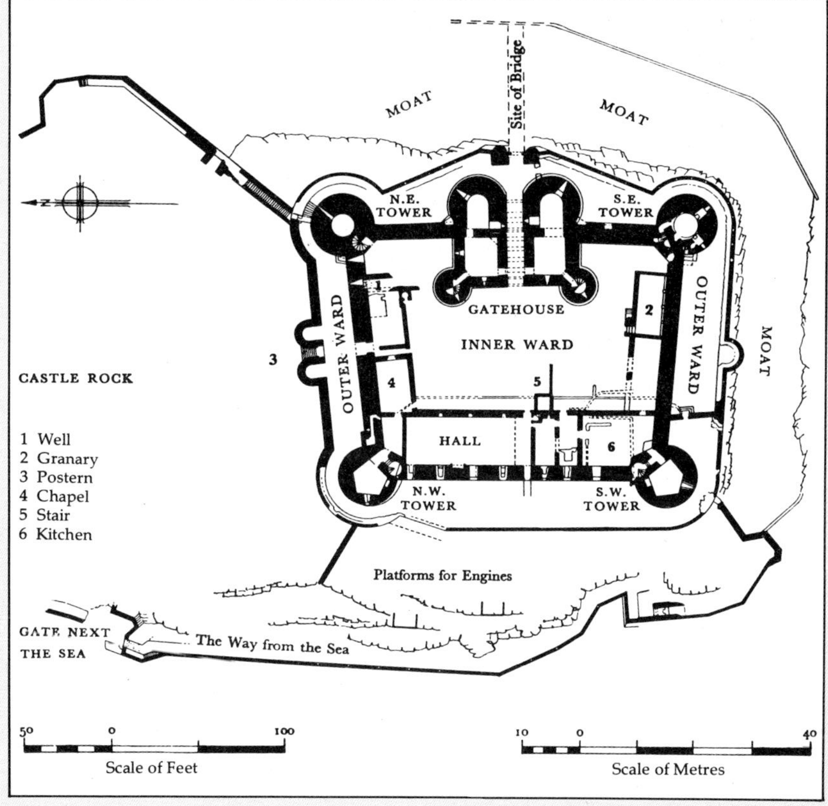

48

49

53 *The castle from across the Seiont*
53 *Y castell dros Afon Seiont*
53 *Vue du Château depuis le Seiont*
53 *Burg von Seiont aus*

51 *The gatehouse from the inner courtyard*
51 *Y tŷ porth o'r cwrt mewnol*
51 *Le corps-de-garde depuis la cour intérieure*
51 *Torhaus – Ansicht vom inneren Burghof*

50 *Reconstruction drawing by Alan Sorrell*
50 *Darlun ailgynhyrchiad gan Alan Sorrell*
50 *Plan de reconstruction par Alan Sorrell*
50 *Rekonstruktionszeichnung von Alan Sorrell*

Glyndŵr and a meeting-place for the parliaments of his supporters. It was held by the Welsh for nearly five years but, at the end of 1408, the castle was retaken by English forces, after a long siege and persistent bombardment by cannon.

Sixty years later, during the Wars of the Roses, Harlech was held for the Lancastrian side by its Welsh constable. Only after a further prolonged siege was it surrendered, in 1468, to the Yorkists, led by William Herbert, Earl of Pembroke. It was the castle's long resistance, after the rest of the country had given in, that provided the inspiration for the song *Men of Harlech*.

52 *View from the south-west*
52 *Golygfa o'r de-orllewin*
52 *Vue du Sud-Ouest*
52 *Ansicht von SW*

50

52

51

Caernarfon
Castle

54 *View from the air*
54 *Golygfa o'r awyr*
54 *Vue aérienne*
54 *Ansicht von oben*

At Caernarfon, King Edward I seems to have been prepared to go to considerable lengths to keep alive its long association, in legend, with the world of imperial Rome and thus, perhaps, endow his own enterprise with a certain authority. The Roman fort of Segontium, on the outskirts of the modern town, may have evoked the mythical tale of the late Roman emperor Magnus Maximus, in the Welsh romances of the *Mabinogion.* This story, which revolves around the personage of Macsen Wledig, tells of his journeying from Rome into a land of high mountains facing an island and seeing a great city with towers of many colours and a chair of ivory with two golden eagles thereon.

Edward's castle at Caernarfon is plainly different from his other foundations, dominating its surroundings by the sheer scale of its fortifications and regal style of architecture. Here, one feels, the king has tried deliberately to recreate, in the reality of stone, that legendary spectacle in the *Mabinogion,* with its eagles and its towers of many colours. For his inspiration, he may have turned to the great walls of Constantinople, the eastern successor to Rome and one of the wonders of the ancient world – there, courses of reddish brown tile variegate its angular towers; here, bands of red sandstone have been used to similar effect. For good measure, high turrets everywhere punctuate Caernarfon's skyline and, on the largest tower, three stone eagles once crowned their battlements to complete the symbolism that is so much in evidence.

54

Caernarfon Castle was built to be the seat of government for the new county of Caernarvonshire and, like Conwy, was linked to a heavily fortified, though smaller, town borough, with high stone walls, towers and gatehouses. The castle, conversely, is very much larger than that of Conwy, rather like an hour-glass in plan and divided into two wards at the narrowest point. Its towers are all polygonal and, on the river front only, are enhanced by coloured stone banding—no doubt a deliberately regal touch—so that, from the oppostive bank of the Seiont, its aspect is truly majestic. What Caernarfon may lack in outer fortifications, however, it makes up for in the multiplicity of defences within that single line of curtain walling. There are two great gatehouses although neither was ever completed: the King's Gate has provision for no fewer than five doors and six portcullises; the Queen's Gate, outside the curcuit of the town walls, would have been approached by way of a high stone-built ramp and drawbridge, rather as at Conwy. The curtain walls are honeycombed by continuous passageways on two levels; these are all well provided with arrow-loops and, on the town side, there are multiple embrasures, so that two or more archers could fire through them simultaneously. Originally, the upper ward was occupied mainly by the earthen mound

55 *The fifth century Roman walls of Constantinople*
55 *Muriau Rhufeinig Caer Gystennin yn y bumed ganrif*
55 *Les murs romains du cinquième siècle de Constantinople*
55 *Römische Stadtmauer in Konstantinopel (5. Jhdt.)*

56 *Caernarfon Castle*
56 *Castell Caernarfon*
56 *Le Château de Caernarfon*
56 *Caernarfon Castle*

55

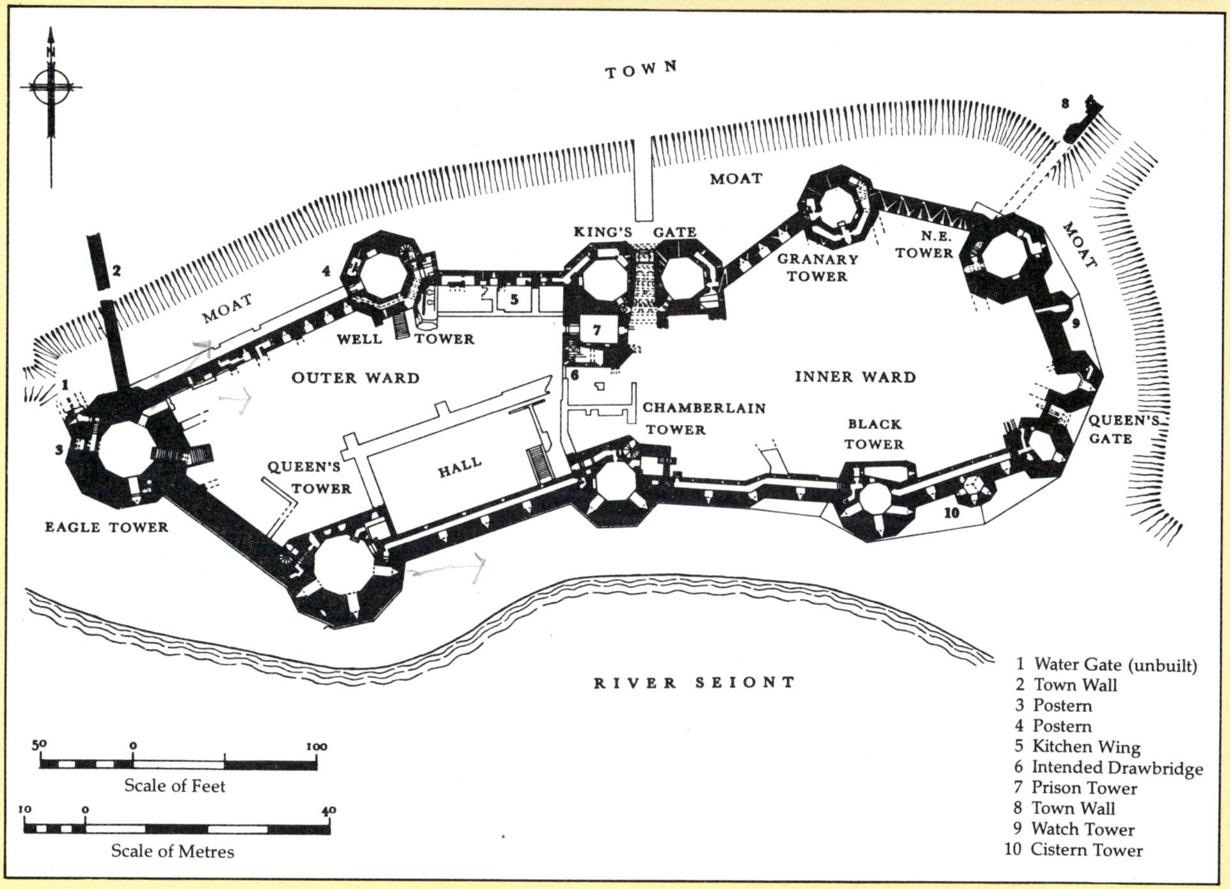

56

TOWN
MOAT
KING'S GATE
GRANARY TOWER
N.E. TOWER
MOAT
WELL TOWER
OUTER WARD
INNER WARD
CHAMBERLAIN TOWER
BLACK TOWER
QUEEN'S GATE
QUEEN'S TOWER
HALL
EAGLE TOWER
RIVER SEIONT

1 Water Gate (unbuilt)
2 Town Wall
3 Postern
4 Postern
5 Kitchen Wing
6 Intended Drawbridge
7 Prison Tower
8 Town Wall
9 Watch Tower
10 Cistern Tower

50 0 100
Scale of Feet

10 0 40
Scale of Metres

57 *Carved stone eagle on the Eagle Tower*
57 *Eryr wedi'i gerfio o garreg ar Dŵr yr Eryr*
57 *Aigle sculpté en pierre situé sur la Tour de l'Aigle*
57 *Adlerskulptur am sogenannten 'Adlerturm' (Eagle Tower)*

58 *The King's Gate*
58 *Porth y Brenin*
58 *La Porte du Roi*
58 *Das 'Königstor' (King's Gate)*

59 *View from the air*
59 *Golygfa o'r awyr*
59 *Vue aérienne*
59 *Ansicht von oben*

57

of an earlier Norman castle motte but in the lower ward were kitchens and other domestic buildings – probably timber-framed structures – and a great hall, which is now completely destroyed.

Edward I's eventual successor, his son Edward, Prince of Wales, was born in temporary buildings within the lower ward in April 1284. Ten years later, a serious revolt broke out in north Wales, led by Madog ap Llywelyn; the half-built castle of Caernarfon and its new town were taken and extensively sacked. After the revolt, the place never again saw such turbulent times and building went slowly on for another 40 years. In 1404, its garrison

59

of 28 successfully held the castle against the well-equipped army of Owain Glyndŵr and his French allies. Surrendered finally in the Civil War, it was afterwards allowed to moulder gently until the last century, when its fortune changed and a programme of comprehensive restoration was undertaken by Sir Llewelyn Turner and his successors. Today, Caernarfon Castle has once again become a fitting place to welcome a Prince of Wales and has been the scene of the ceremonial investiture of the last two Princes in 1911 and 1969.

58

Beaumaris
Castle

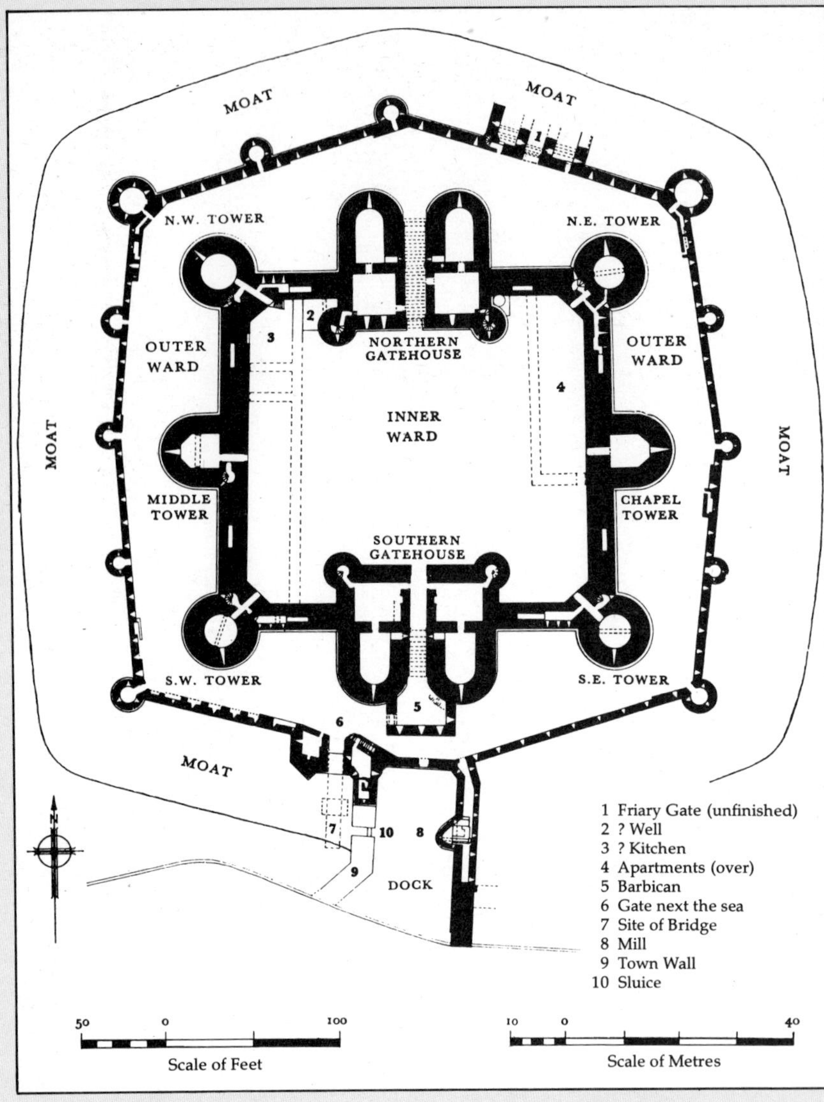

60

60 *Beaumaris Castle*
60 *Castell Biwmares*
60 *Le Château de Beaumaris*
60 *Beaumaris Castle*

A castle on Anglesey was almost certainly planned by King Edward I when he visited the island in 1283 and designated the Welsh town of Llanfaes to be its seat of government. Llanfaes was the natural site for a new military foundation, for it was already the principal trading port and ferrying point for traffic to the mainland. Resources, however, were already stretched to the limit elsewhere and execution of the scheme was postponed until a more opportune moment. That moment arrived a little sooner, perhaps, than the king had anticipated, for in the autumn of 1294, the Welsh in the north rose against their conscription for military service in Gascony. The rebels' main success was against Caernarfon but, by late spring 1295, the revolt was crushed after an arduous winter campaign and, in the king's estimation, the time was now ripe for the commencement of his deferred castle. By royal decree, the Welsh population of Llanfaes was evicted to the fresh settlement of Newborough, in the south of the island while, on the *fair marsh* beside the old town, the new castle and town of Beaumaris were begun.

In sole charge of the project was Master James of St George, who must now have been aged around sixty and had seven major castles already to his credit in Wales. One of his first tasks, on taking command, was the building of a second bridge over to the mainland, to replace the ill-fated earlier bridge of boats destroyed in 1283. Labour and building materials were thus brought across to Anglesey, together with the king's main army, early in April 1295. During that first season, the castle of Beaumaris received the largest single injection of finance of any site in north Wales; by the end of it, £6,736 had been spent here. The labour force too was enormous, averaging around 2,600 men over the same period – some 1,800 of them alone were diggers, whose wages came to £1,468 12s. In July of that year, the king came to stay at Beaumaris to inspect his latest project and for two evenings, so the Exchequer records tell us, he was entertained in the midst of the new building works by the music of an

61

62

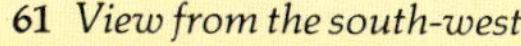

61 *View from the south-west*
61 *Golygfa o'r de-orllewin*
61 *Vue du Sud-Ouest*
61 *Ansicht von SW*

62 *Reconstruction drawing by Alan Sorrell*
62 *Darlun, ailgynhyrchiad gan Alan Sorrell*
62 *Plan de reconstruction par Alan Sorrell*
62 *Rekonstruktionszeichnung von Alan Sorrell*

63 *The north gatehouse*
63 *Tŷ porth y gogledd*
63 *Corps-de-garde du Nord*
63 *Nördl. Torhaus*

63

English harpist, one Adam of Clitheroe.

Beaumaris was a green-field site, unencumbered by any natural or man-made obstacles, but also without any material aids to defence. Here, Master James has created the ultimate concentric plan; it relies totally upon its own defences and is symmetrical in layout. The castle is surrounded by a water-filled moat, incorporating a tidal dock for ships to tie up (an iron ring for this purpose can still

be seen fixed in the wall). Across the moat, a low outer wall is punctuated by 16 towers and two gates and, beyond this, lies the heart of the castle, its great curtain walls protected by two enormous gateways and a further six towers. Here, one feels, the final goal of defence has been attained; it was practically impossible to take by storm and, with a protected dock for shipping, unlikely to be starved into submission. At either side of the inner ward there is evidence for building ranges that are either now demolished or, possibly, were never built – service areas to the west and, to the east, a hall and private accommodation which gave access to the fine chapel in the central tower. As at Caernarfon, the curtain walls are pierced by continuous passageways, for communication as well as added defence.

Events outside Wales, however, were to overtake the building of Beaumaris. Campaigns in Gascony and Scotland began to siphon off capital finance and resources from 1296 onwards: in 1298, a major constitutional crisis at home caused them to dry up altogether with the outer wall only half finished and the great inner towers, which seem to have been intended to bear a veritable forest of castellated turrets, part built. From, 1306 until 1330, building carried on, but little was accomplished in all that time save the completion of the outer wall and the erection of a protective barbican for the inner gatehouse. Although incomplete, the castle was garrisoned throughout its uneventful life until the Civil War, when it was finally surrendered to Parliament in 1646.

64 *The chapel*
64 *Y capel*
64 *La chapelle*
64 *Kapelle*

Printed in U.K. for HMSO
Dd. 717399 C. 550